SCANDALOUS

Other Re:Lit Books:

Re:Lit: Vintage Jesus:

Vintage Jesus

Vintage Church

Death by Love

Religion Saves

Doctrine

Re:Lit: A Book You'll Actually Read

On Church Leadership

On the New Testament

On the Old Testament

On Who Is God?

SCANDALOUS

The Cross and Resurrection
of Jesus

D. A. Carson

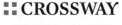

CROSSWAY

WHEATON, ILLINOIS

Scandalous: The Cross and Resurrection of Jesus

Copyright © 2010 by D. A. Carson

Published by Crossway
        a publishing ministry of Good News Publishers
        1300 Crescent Street
        Wheaton, Illinois 60187

Art Direction and Design: Patrick Mahoney of The Mahoney Design Team

First printing 2010

Printed in the United States of America

Unless otherwise indicated, Scripture references are from *The Holy Bible: New International Version*®. Copyright © 1973, 1978, 1984 by International Bible Society. Used by permission of Zondervan Publishing House. All rights reserved.

The "NIV" and "New International Version" trademarks are registered in the United States Patent and Trademark Office by International Bible Society. Use of either trademark requires the permission of International Bible Society.

All emphases in Scripture quotations have been added by the author.

Trade paperback ISBN: 978-1-4335-1125-7

PDF ISBN: 978-1-4335-1126-4

Mobipocket ISBN: 978-1-4335-1127-1

EPub ISBN: 978-1-4335-2378-6

Library of Congress Cataloging-in-Publication Data
Carson, D. A.
  Scandalous : the cross and resurrection of Jesus / D. A. Carson.
    p. cm.
  ISBN 978-1-4335-1125-7 (tpb)
    1. Jesus Christ—Crucifixion—Biblical teaching. 2. Jesus Christ—
Resurrection—Biblical teaching. I. Title.
BT453.C28   2010
232—dc22   2009030131

VP		19	18	17	16	15	14	13	12	11	10
13	12	11	10	9	8	7	6	5	4	3	2	1

"What happens when one of the world's preeminent theologians expounds on some of the Bible's prominent texts? This book."
— MARK DRISCOLL, Pastor, Mars Hill Church, Seattle; President, Acts 29 Church Planting Network

"Don Carson's clarity in communicating Scripture is a great gift, and in this book, he gives it to us. This professor can preach! These are model messages on crucial passages. They are delicious meditations that instruct our minds and feed our souls. Biblical content—straight, ripped, hard, solid—this is what Carson gives us about Christ's cross and resurrection. Read, mark, learn, and inwardly digest."
— MARK DEVER, Senior Pastor, Capitol Hill Baptist Church, Washington DC

"This is vintage Carson—informed exegesis and engaging exposition, theologically rich and devotionally warm, lucid, insightful, probing. God's truth glows! Don Carson shows us what the Bible is for, and his words make me want to preach the scandalous cross of Christ with greater passion."
— BILL KYNES, Pastor, Cornerstone Evangelical Free Church, Annandale, Virginia

"There is no Christianity apart from the death of Christ on the cross and his resurrection from the dead. Carson helps us to more clearly understand the passion of the cross and the triumph of the resurrection. What a gift to every follower of Christ. As you read through these pages you will be moved to worship the Lamb that was slain!"
— CRAWFORD W. LORITTS JR., author; speaker; Senior Pastor, Fellowship Bible Church, Roswell, Georgia.

"Don Carson has provided a rich, thoughtful, and theologically honest introduction of the person and work of Jesus. With the biblical fidelity, clarity, and wisdom we have come to expect from his writings, Carson provides a treatment of the ironies of the cross not merely as a literary device but as a powerful analysis of the subversive, upside-down nature of the cross; namely, the powerful, redeeming, trusting king of the universe becoming a powerless, marginalized, and crucified savior. He believes that Jesus cried this cry, 'My God! I am forsaken!' so that for all eternity we will not have to. We are grateful for Carson's fruitful labors in showing us the irony of the mocked king who really is the King, not only for the Jews but also for the entire world."

—STEPHEN T. UM, Senior Minister, Citylife Presbyterian Church, Boston; President, Center for Gospel Culture

To
JoyJoy

Contents

Preface

Nothing is more central to the Bible than Jesus' death and resurrection. The entire Bible pivots on one weekend in Jerusalem about two thousand years ago. Attempts to make sense of the Bible that do not give prolonged thought to integrating the crucifixion and resurrection of Jesus are doomed to failure, at best exercises in irrelevance. Jesus' own followers did not expect him to be crucified; they certainly did not expect him to rise again. Yet after these events their thinking and attitudes were so transformed that they could see the sheer inevitability that Jesus would die on a cross and leave an empty tomb behind, and absolutely everything in their lives was changed.

However much the Bible insists on the historicity of these events, it never treats them as mere pieces of raw data—admittedly, rather surprising raw data—the meaning of which we are free to make up for ourselves. It is as important to know what these events mean as to know that they happened.

This little book is a modest attempt to summarize not only what happened but also what they mean—in short, to provide an introductory explanation of the cross and resurrection. I do this by unpacking what some of the earliest witnesses of Jesus' death and resurrection wrote. The words of those witnesses are preserved in the Bible; the chapters in this book are explanations of five sections of the Bible that get at these questions.

Over the years I've had occasion to unpack many parts of the Bible that herald Jesus' death and resurrection. In December 2008 I gave these five addresses at a Resurgence conference in Mars Hill, Seattle. I am grateful to Mark Driscoll and the folks at the Henry Center for putting the conference together. And I am especially grateful to Andy Naselli for proofing this manuscript and compiling the indexes that make the written form of these talks a little more useful than they might otherwise have been.

—D. A. Carson
Trinity Evangelical Divinity School

Then the governor's soldiers took Jesus into the Praetorium and gathered the whole company of soldiers around him. They stripped him and put a scarlet robe on him, and then twisted together a crown of thorns and set it on his head. They put a staff in his right hand and knelt in front of him and mocked him. "Hail, king of the Jews!" they said. They spit on him, and took the staff and struck him on the head again and again. After they had mocked him, they took off the robe and put his own clothes on him. Then they led him away to crucify him.

—MATTHEW 27:27–31

1
The Ironies of the Cross

Matthew 27:27–51a

He was, on the whole, a very good king. He united the disparate tribes, built a nation, and established a dynasty. Personally courageous, he also built a formidable defense system and secured his country's borders. He proved to be an able administrator, and on the whole he ruled with justice. As if that were not enough, he was an accomplished poet and musician.

But in his middle years, he seduced a young woman next door. To understand a little more how perverse this evil was, we must recall that this young woman's husband was at that time away from home, at the military front, fighting the king's battles. Out of this one-night stand, the woman became pregnant and sent word to the king. He was a "fixer," and he thought he could fix this. He sent a messenger to the front, asking the military command to send the young man back to the capital with an ostensible message for the king. The young man came, of course, but as it turned out, he didn't return home to sleep with his wife: somehow he felt that would be letting down the side with his mates back at the front. The young man merely slept in the royal courtyard, ready to head back to the front—and King David knew he would be found out. So he sent back a secret message to the commanding officers at the front, a message carried by the hand of this young man, a message that was his death warrant. The officers were to arrange a skirmish, with everyone in the unit except the young man given a secret signal when to withdraw. The inevitable happened: the unit withdrew, and the young man was left alone in the skirmish and killed. Shortly after, the king married the pregnant widow. David thought he had gotten away with his sin.

God sent the prophet Nathan to confront him. Faithful prophet though he was, Nathan decided he'd better approach the monarch with suitable caution, so he began with a story. He said, in effect, "Your majesty, I've come across a difficult case up country. There are two farmers, neighbors. One is filthy rich; the number of animals in his herds and flocks is past counting. The other chap is a subsistence farmer. He has one little lamb, that's all. In fact, he doesn't even have that lamb any more. Some visitors dropped by the home of the rich man, who, instead of showing appropriate hospitality by killing one of the animals from his own flocks and preparing a feast, went and stole the one little lamb owned by the dirt farmer. What do you think should be done about this?"

David was outraged. He said, "As surely as the LORD lives, the man who did this must die! He must pay for that lamb four times over, because he did such a thing and had no pity" (2 Sam. 12:5–6). David had no idea how painfully ironic his utterance was. Nathan knew, of course, and the writer knew, and God knew, and the readers know—but David could not detect the desperate irony of his own words until Nathan said, "You are the man!" (v. 7).

We all know what irony is. Irony expresses meaning by using words that normally mean the opposite of what is actually being said. Sometimes the irony is intentional, of course: the speaker knows he is using irony; at other times, as here, David hasn't a clue that his words are ironic until his hypocrisy is exposed. He thinks his words establish him as a principled judge who makes right and fair judicial decisions, but in the light of his secret life he merely exposes himself as a wretched hypocrite. The real meaning of the words, in this broader context, is a blistering condemnation of the very man who thinks that by using these words he is showing himself to be a just man and a good king.

Some irony is vicious, of course; some is hilariously funny. But we all know that irony has the potential, especially in narrative, for bringing a situation into sharp focus. Very often it is the irony in the narrative that enables hearers and readers to see what is really going on. Irony provides a dimension of depth and color that would otherwise be missing.

Of the New Testament writers, those most given to irony are Matthew and John. In the passage before us, Matthew unfolds what takes place as Jesus is crucified—but he does so by displaying four huge ironies that show attentive readers what is *really* going on.

Permit me to remind you of the context. By this point, Jesus has been in the public eye for two or three years, the years of his public ministry. Now, however, he has fallen foul of the religious and political authorities. They resent his popularity, they fear his potential political power, they are suspicious of his motives. They wonder if the rising number of his followers could turn into a rebellion against the reigning superpower of the day, the mighty Roman Empire—for there could be only one outcome in a conflict with Rome. So Jesus has to be crushed. They provide a kangaroo court, find Jesus guilty of treason, and manage to secure the sanction of the Roman governor to have Jesus executed by crucifixion. All of this, they thought, was politically expedient, religiously for the best.

And here in the text (Matt. 27:27), we pick up the account immediately after sentence has been passed. In those days there was no long delay on death row for the prisoner. Once a capital sentence was handed down, the prisoner was taken out and executed within a few hours or at most a few days. In the text before us, we find the soldiers preparing Jesus for immediate crucifixion. As Matthew tells the story, we learn to reflect on four profound ironies of the cross.

The Man Who Is Mocked as King Is the King (Matt. 27:27–31)

Apparently Jesus had been flogged earlier, as part of his interrogation. Immediately after sentence of crucifixion was passed, Jesus was flogged again (v. 26). This too was standard procedure; it was customary to flog prisoners before taking them out to be crucified. But what takes place in verses 27 to 31 is *not* standard procedure. It is more like barracks-room humor. The governor's soldiers gather around, strip Jesus of his clothes, and drape some sort of scarlet robe on him, pretending he is a royal figure. Then they wind together some strands of vine thorns, the spikes of which are 15 to 20 cm. long. They crunch this down on his head to make a cruel crown of thorns. They put a staff into his hand and pretend it is a scepter. Alternately bowing before Jesus in mock reverence and hitting him in brutal cruelty, they cry, "Hail, king of the Jews!"—and complete the acclamation by spitting in his face and hitting him again and again with the mock scepter. Raucous, mocking laughter keeps the room alive until the soldiers tire of their sport. They have finished laughing at him as the king of the Jews. Now they put his own clothes back on him and lead him away to be crucified.

But Matthew knows, and the readers know, and God knows, that Jesus *is* the king of the Jews. In case we've missed the theme, Matthew reminds us of it twice more in the following verses: the *titulus*, the charge against Jesus, is nailed to the cross above his head: "THIS IS JESUS, THE KING OF THE JEWS" (v. 37). The mockers are still dismissing him as the king of Israel in verse 42. More importantly, Matthew has already made the theme clear throughout his Gospel. His very first verse reads, "This is of the genealogy of Jesus Christ *the son of David*, the son of Abraham" (1:1). The ensuing genealogy is broken up somewhat artificially into three fourteens, the central fourteen covering the years in which the Davidic dynasty reigned in Jerusalem. Even the number fourteen is a code for the name "David." All the OT promises that look forward to the coming Davidic king spring from 2 Samuel 7, anchored in David's life about 1000 B.C. Almost three hundred years later, the prophet Isaiah anticipates one who will sit on the throne of his father David, but who would also be called "Wonderful Counselor, Mighty God, Everlasting Father, Prince of Peace" (Isa. 9:6). Matthew's opening chapter picks up on this Old Testament anticipation. In the second chapter, the Magi ask, "Where is the one who has been born king of the Jews?" (2:2). As he begins his public ministry, Jesus talks constantly about the kingdom—its nature, dawning, promise, and consummation. In some of the so-called "parables of the kingdom," the stories Jesus tells sometimes make Jesus himself out to be the king. The same theme is raised in the trial before Pilate. In 27:11, Pilate the governor asks Jesus, "Are you the king of the Jews?" "Yes, it is as you say," Jesus replies, yet the form of his response, while affirmative, depicts a gentle hesitation, because Jesus knows full well he is *not* a king in any way that Pilate fears. His reign does not spell out military threat to Caesar. Pilate himself soon discerns that even if Jesus claims to be the king of the Jews, he poses no immediate political threat, and he seeks to have him released. Still, the confession is there, and Jesus stands condemned on the capital charge of treason.

And while the soldiers mock Jesus as the king of the Jews, transparently Matthew knows, and his readers know, and God knows, that Jesus *is* the king of the Jews.

Indeed, look closely and you will see *two* layers of irony. The mockery of the soldiers was *meant* to be ironic. When they exclaim, "Hail, king of the Jews!" what they mean is the exact opposite: Jesus is *not* the king but a rather pathetic criminal. Doubtless the soldiers think their humor is deliciously ironic. But Matthew sees an even deeper irony; in fact, while the soldiers demean Jesus as a pathetic criminal, the words they use actually tell the truth, the opposite of what they mean: Jesus really *is* the king. That is the point of this paragraph: the man who is mocked as king—is the king (vv. 27–31).

Those who know their Bibles well know that Jesus is *more* than king of the Jews: he is king over all, he is Lord over all. Matthew himself makes this clear in his closing verses. This side of the resurrection, Jesus declares that all authority in heaven and on earth is his (28:18); his authority is none less than the authority of God. He is king of the universe. He is king over the soldiers who mock him. He is king over you and me. And one day, Paul assures us, every knee will bow, and every tongue will confess that Jesus is Lord. The man who is mocked as king—is the king.

But we must probe a little further. With what conception of kingship is Jesus operating? In the first century, no one entertained the notion of a constitutional monarchy, like that of Great Britain, where the monarch has almost no real authority apart from moral suasion. In the ancient world, kings *reigned*. That's what kings did; that's how they operated. Indeed, that is the notion of kingship until fairly recent times. Louis XIV was not a constitutional monarch in the current British sense. What kind of king, then, is Jesus, in Matthew's mind, if Jesus is going to death on a cross? Is he a failed king?

Once again, Matthew has already given us some insight into the reality of Jesus' kingship. We must scan the interesting exchange in Matthew 20:20–28. The mother of the apostles James and John approaches Jesus, along with her two sons, requesting a favor. "What is it you want?" he asks. She replies, "Grant that one of these two sons of mine may sit at your right and the other at your left *in your kingdom*" (v. 21). Clearly they anticipated that Jesus would sit as king in a quite normal, historical, physical sense, and make his apostles the members of his cabinet, and they were hoping that James and John would get the two top jobs—secretary of state and secretary of defense, perhaps. Jesus tells them, in effect, that they have no idea what they are asking for: "Can you drink the cup I am going to drink?" he asks, referring, of course, to his impending suffering. With supreme overconfidence and massive ignorance, they reply, "We can" (v. 22). You can almost imagine Jesus smiling inwardly: well, yes, in one sense, they will participate in his cup, his cup of suffering: one of the two brothers, James, would become the first apostolic martyr, and the other would die as an exile on Patmos. Still, it is not Jesus' role to dispense the right to sit on his left or his right: that role the Father has reserved for himself.

When the ten other apostles hear of the request of James and John and their mother, they are incensed—not, of course, because of the arrogance and impertinence of their request, but because the ten did not get their requests in first. So Jesus calls the Twelve together, and gives us one of the most important insights into the nature of the kingdom. He says: "You know that the rulers of the Gentiles lord it over them, and their high officials exercise authority over them. Not so with you. Instead, whoever wants to become great among you must be your servant, and whoever wants to be first must be your slave—just as the Son of Man did not come to be served, but to serve, and to give his life as a ransom for many" (vv. 25–28). This profound utterance must not be misunderstood. Jesus does not mean that there is *no* sense in which he exercises authority. Transparently, that is not the case—and in the closing verses Matthew reminds us, as we have seen, that Jesus claims all authority in heaven and on earth. What he means, rather, is something like this. The kings and rulers and presidents of this fallen world order exercise their authority out of a deep sense of self-promotion, out of a deep sense of wanting to be number one, out of a deep sense of self-preservation, even out of a deep sense of entitlement. By contrast, Jesus exercises his authority in such a way as to seek the good of his subjects, and that takes him, finally, to the cross. He did not come to be served, as if that were an end in itself; even in his sovereign mission he comes to serve—to give his life a ransom for many. Those who exercise any authority at any level in the kingdom in which Jesus is king must serve the same way—not with implicit demands of self-promotion, confidence in their right to rule, or a desire to sit at Jesus' right hand or his left hand, but with a passion to serve.

Small wonder, then, that Pilate could not figure Jesus out. Jesus claimed to be king, but he had none of the pretensions of the monarchs of this world. Small wonder that for the next three hundred years, Christians would speak, with profound irony, of Jesus reigning from the cross.

So here is the first irony in Matthew's presentation of Jesus' crucifixion: the man who is mocked as king—is the king.

The Man Who Is Utterly Powerless Is Powerful (Matt. 27:32–40)

I cannot take the time to deal with all the subtle details in Matthew's text. What is transparent is that Matthew provides ample evidence to demonstrate just how weak and powerless Jesus is. In the Roman world, the upright of the cross, the vertical member, was usually left in the ground at the place of crucifixion—usually near a public crossroads or thoroughfare so that as many people as possible could witness the torment and learn to fear Roman power. The horizontal member was carried by the victim out to the place of crucifixion. There the victim was tied or nailed to this cross-member, which was then hoisted up and suspended from the upright. But Jesus is now so weak he cannot even manage to carry this chunk of wood on his shoulder to the place of execution. So the soldiers exercise their legal right to conscript a bystander for the task, and Simon from Cyrene is forced to do the work (v. 32). Victims were crucified completely naked: the cross was meant to be an instrument of shame as well as of pain. So the soldiers gamble to determine who will gain possession of Jesus' clothing (v. 35). It is difficult to imagine a portrait more calculated to depict Jesus' utter powerlessness.

"And sitting down, [the soldiers] kept watch over him there" (v. 36). At a slightly earlier time in the history of the Roman Empire, soldiers had sometimes crucified people and then walked away to let them die. In some known instances, friends of the victim had lifted him down from the cross—and the victim had survived. So by this stage in Roman history, it was imperial policy to post soldiers at a crucifixion site until death had taken place. That is what is depicted in verse 36: the soldiers keep watch over Jesus. Jesus has no hope, none whatsoever, of rescue. Suffering immeasurably, shamed intolerably, broken in body and spirit, without any prospect except the release of death, Jesus hangs in shame on that wretched cross, utterly powerless.

Then comes the mockery that shows the significance of this list of evidences attesting Jesus' weakness and powerlessness. We are told that some who passed by hurled insults at him and said, "You who are going to destroy the temple and build it in three days, save yourself! Come down from the cross, if you are the Son of God!" (vv. 39–40).

If we are going to understand why Matthew reports these words, we must remember that the theme of Jesus' destruction of the temple has already been introduced. Earlier in Jesus' trial, this time before the high priest, the authorities were still scrambling to find suitable witnesses who could destroy Jesus. In Matthew 26:61 we are told that two witnesses finally came forward who charged, "This fellow said, 'I am able to destroy the temple of God and rebuild it in three days.'" This charge was potentially very dangerous. The Romans were worried about conflicts between peoples of different religions, so they made it a capital offense to desecrate a temple, any temple. If Jesus' words about destroying the temple of God could be taken as a serious intention to harm a temple, then they had him. But that line of thought peters out in Matthew 26; from parallel accounts, we learn that the witnesses couldn't get their stories straight. Eventually Jesus was condemned on a treason charge, rather than on a desecration-of-a-temple charge.

But what fun Jesus' words afforded to the mockers! He had glibly talked about destroying and rebuilding the temple in three days. What kind of power would that require? With modern technology, we can put together a prefabricated house in a day or two; we can build a skyscraper in a year or two. Historically, however, this kind of speed is a very recent development. None of the great cathedrals of Europe was ever seen in its fully constructed form by its original architect; building a cathedral took longer than one lifetime. The builders of the temple in Jerusalem faced additional constraints: they were not to use a mason's hammer anywhere near temple precincts. Each of the great stones had to be measured and cut elsewhere, and then brought in by animal and human power, without help of hydraulics. Yet here was Jesus, glibly talking about destroying and building a temple in three days. What kind of power would that take? What kind of *supernatural* power would that take? Yet here Jesus hangs, utterly powerless, on a Roman cross. The sting of the mockery turns on this bitter contrast between Jesus' claims to power and his current transparent powerlessness. Once again, the mockers think they are indulging in fine irony. Jesus claimed so much power, so very much power; now witness his powerlessness. So in the light of his claim, they say "save yourself"—which of course they utter ironically, since they are convinced he is helpless and cannot do a thing to help himself. Jesus' claims are somewhere between ridiculous and scandalous—and they deserve to be mocked.

But the apostles know, and the readers of the Gospels know, and God knows, that Jesus' demonstration of power is displayed precisely in the weakness of the cross. Because we read John's Gospel, especially John 2, we know what Jesus actually said on this subject: "Destroy this temple, and I will raise it again in three days" (2:19). According to John, Jesus' opponents did not have a clue what he meant; indeed, Jesus' own disciples had no idea, at the time, what he meant. But after Jesus was raised from the dead, John says, the disciples remembered his words; they believed the Scripture and the words Jesus had spoken. They knew he was talking *about his body* (vv. 20–22). The point is that under the terms of the old covenant, the temple was the great meeting place between a holy God and his sinful people. This was the place of sacrifice, the place of atonement for sin. But this side of the cross, where Jesus by his sacrifice pays for our sin, Jesus himself becomes the great meeting place between a holy God and his sinful people; thus he becomes the temple, the meeting place between God and his people. It is not as if Jesus in his incarnation adequately serves as the temple of God. That is a huge mistake. Jesus says, "*Destroy* this temple, and in three days I will raise it up." It is in Jesus' death, in his destruction, and in his resurrection three days later, that Jesus meets our needs and reconciles us to God, becoming the temple, the supreme meeting place between God and sinners. To use Paul's language, we do not simply preach Christ; rather, we preach Christ crucified.

Here is the glory, the paradox, the irony; here, once again, there are two levels of irony. The mockers think they are witty and funny as they mock Jesus' pretensions and laugh at his utter weakness after he has claimed he could destroy the temple and raise it in three days. But the apostles know, and the readers know, and God knows, that there is a deeper irony: it is precisely *by staying on the cross in abject powerlessness* that Jesus establishes himself as the temple and comes to the resurrection in fullness of power. The only way Jesus will save himself, and save his people, is by hanging on that wretched cross, in utter powerlessness. The words the mockers use to hurl insults and condescending sneers actually describe what is bringing about the salvation of the Lord.

The man who is utterly powerless—is powerful.

This principle has already been worked over by Matthew. According to Matthew 16, at Caesarea Philippi Jesus asks his disciples who they think he is. Simon Peter answers, "You are the Christ, the Son of the living God" (v. 16). We must not interpret Peter's confession too generously. When *we* say, "Jesus is the Christ," we inevitably include in the confession the substance of Jesus' person, his crucifixion, his resurrection, for we live this side of those great events. We cannot think of him without thinking of his cross and resurrection. But when Peter confesses to Jesus, "You are the Christ," he includes nothing of the crucifixion and resurrection. By "Christ," he has in mind a conquering, victorious, messianic, Davidic, king. The proof lies in the following verses. When in the wake of Peter's confession, Jesus goes on to talk about his impending suffering, death, and resurrection (v. 21), Peter still has no category by which to understand what Jesus is saying. Messiahs do not die; they win! They are not crucified; they conquer! So Peter takes it on himself to rebuke Jesus smartly: "'Never, Lord!' he said. 'This shall never happen to you!'" (v. 22). So flawed is Peter's understanding of Jesus' purposes in coming as the Messiah that he earns the Master's immortal rebuke, "Get behind me, Satan! You are a stumbling block to me; you do not have in mind the things of God, but the things of men" (v. 23).

It is at this juncture that Jesus universalizes the principle that is at stake: "If anyone would come after me," he says, "he must deny himself and take up his cross and follow me. For whoever wants to save his life will lose it, but whoever loses his life for me will find it" (vv. 24–25). This expression "to take up one's cross" is not an idiom by which to refer to some trivial annoyance—an ingrown toenail, perhaps, or a toothache, or an awkward in-law: "We all have our crosses to bear." No, in the first century, that sort of interpretation would have been impossible. In the first century it was as culturally unthinkable to make jokes about crucifixion as it would be today to make jokes about Auschwitz. To take up your cross does not mean to move forward with courage despite the fact you lost your job or your spouse. It means you are under sentence of death; you are taking up the horizontal cross-member on your way to the place of crucifixion. You have abandoned all hope of life in this world. And then, Jesus says, and only then, are we ready to follow him.

Is this not universal Christian teaching? It is in dying that we live; it is in denying ourselves that we find ourselves; it is in giving that we receive. Paul understands the same principle when he says, in 2 Corinthians 12, that he has learned to rejoice when he is weak, for when he is weak, he experiences God's strength.

All of this, of course, was first of all supremely exemplified in the Lord Jesus. In shame, ignominy, and powerlessness he died in suffering and agony and rose in power to become the risen temple of God, the living meeting place between God and his people. The mockers laugh at their perception of the irony of the situation: Jesus made such outrageous claims to power, claiming he could destroy the temple and build it again in three days, when in fact he dies in the throes of the most abysmal weakness. But we see a deeper irony: the very weakness the mockers find amusing is Jesus' own way to power, the way to the resurrection, the way to functioning as the mighty temple of the living God. Although our own death to self-interest never functions with the same atoning significance as the death of Jesus, the same principle applies to us: in dying we live, in denying ourselves we find ourselves, as we take up our cross and follow Jesus.

Here, then, is Matthew's second irony of the cross: the man who is utterly powerless—is powerful.

The Man Who Can't Save Himself Saves Others (Matt. 27:41–42)

The mockery continues in verses 41and 42: "In the same way [that is, with similar mockery] the chief priests, the teachers of the law and the elders mocked him. 'He saved others,' they said, 'but he can't save himself! He's the king of Israel! Let him come down now from the cross, and we will believe in him.'"

What do we mean today by the verb *to save*? Ask someone at random on the streets of Seattle what the verb "to save" means, and what will be the response? Someone who is worried about his financial portfolio may reply, "'Save' is what you'd better do if you want money set aside for a comfortable retirement." Ask a sports fan what the verb means, and he may reply, "'Save' is what a fine goalie does; he stops the ball from going into the net, and thus *saves* the point." Ask computer techies what the verb means, and they will surely tell you that you jolly well better *save* your data by backing it up frequently, for otherwise when your computer crashes you may lose everything.

The mockers in verses 41 and 42 do not mean any of these things, of course. They are saying that apparently Jesus "saved" many other people—he healed the sick, he exorcised demons, he fed the hungry; occasionally he even raised the dead—but now he could not "save" himself from execution. He could not be much of a savior after all. Thus even their formal affirmation that Jesus "saved" others is uttered with irony in a context that undermines his ability. This would-be savior is a disappointment and a failure, and the mockers enjoy their witty sneering.

But once again, the mockers speak better than they know. Matthew knows, and the readers know, and God knows, that in one profound sense if Jesus is to save others, he really cannot save himself.

We must begin with the way Matthew himself introduces the verb *to save*. It first shows up in Matthew's first chapter. God tells Joseph that the baby in his fiancée's womb has been engendered by the Holy Spirit. God further instructs him, "She will give birth to a son, and you are to give him the name Jesus, because he will *save* his people from their sins" (1:21). "Jesus" is the Greek form of "Joshua," which, roughly, means "YHWH saves." With this meaning so placarded at the beginning of his Gospel, Matthew gives his readers insight into Jesus the Messiah's mission by reporting why God himself assigned this name: Jesus has come to save his people from their sins.

The entire Gospel must be read with this opening announcement in mind. If in Matthew 2 the infant Jesus in some ways recapitulates the descent of Israel into Egypt, it is part of his self-identity with them, for he came to save his people from their sins. If he experiences temptation at the hand of Satan himself, and repeatedly triumphs over it, it is because he must show *himself* removed from sin, however tempted, if he is to save his people from *their* sins. If in Matthew 5–7, in what we call the Sermon on the Mount, Jesus gives matchless and finely woven material on what life in the kingdom of heaven is like and how it fulfills Old Testament anticipation, it is, in part, because transformation of the lives of sinful human beings is part and parcel of Jesus' mission: he came to save his people from their sins, as much the practice of sin as its guilt. If in chapters 8 and 9 Matthew reports a variety of symbol-laden miracles of healing and power, it is because the reversal of disease and the destruction of the demonic are inevitable components of saving his people from their sins. That is why Matthew 8:17 cites Isaiah 53:4: "He took up our infirmities and carried our diseases"—for his name is Jesus, YHWH saves, and he came to save his people from their sins. If Matthew 10 reports a trainee mission, this is part of the preparation for the extension of Jesus' earthly ministry into the future, when the good news of the gospel, the gospel of the kingdom, will be preached in all the world, for Jesus came to save his people from their sins. In this fashion we could work our way through every chapter of Matthew's Gospel and learn the same lesson again and again: Jesus came to save his people from their sins. *Principle*

Matthew knows this, the readers know this, God knows this. They know that Jesus is hanging on this damnable cross because he came to save his people from their sins. Even the words of institution at the Last Supper prepare us to understand the significance of Jesus' blood, shed on the cross: "This is my blood of the covenant, which is poured out for many *for the forgiveness of sins*" (26:28). To use the language of Peter, Jesus died, the just for the unjust, to bring us to God; to use Jesus' own language, he came to give his life a ransom for many.

When I was a boy I had a very perverse imagination, even more perverse, I suspect, than it is now. I sometimes liked to read a story, stop at some crucial point in the narrative, and wonder how the plot would unfold if certain crucial determining points were changed. My favorite biblical story for this doubtful exercise was the account of the crucifixion of Jesus. The mockers cry with irony and sarcasm, "He saved others, but he can't save himself. He's the King of Israel! Let him come down now from the cross, and we will believe in him." In my mind's eye, I could see Jesus gathering his strength, and suddenly leaping down from the cross, healed, demanding clothes.

What would happen? How would the narrative now develop?

Would they believe in him?

At one level, of course, they certainly would: this would be a pretty remarkable and convincing display of power, and the mockers would be back-peddling pretty fast. But in the full Christian sense, would they believe in him? Of course not! To believe in Jesus in the Christian sense means not less than trusting him utterly as the One who has borne our sin in his own body on the tree, as the One whose life and death and resurrection, offered up in our place, has reconciled us to God. If Jesus had leapt off the cross, the mockers and other onlookers could *not* have believed in Jesus in *that* sense, because he would not have sacrificed himself for us, so there would be nothing to trust, except our futile and empty self-righteousness.

Suddenly the words of the mockers take on a new weight of meaning. "He saved others," they said, "but he can't save himself." The deeper irony is that, in a way they did not understand, they were speaking the truth. If he had saved himself, he could not have saved others; the only way he could save others was precisely by not saving himself. In the irony behind the irony that the mockers intended, they spoke the truth they themselves did not see. The man who can't save himself—saves others.

One of the reasons they were so blind is that they thought in terms of merely physical restraints. When they said "he can't save himself," they meant that the nails held him there, the soldiers prevented any possibility of rescue, his powerlessness and weakness guaranteed his death. For them, the words "he can't save himself" expressed a physical impossibility. But those who know who Jesus is are fully aware that nails and soldiers cannot stand in the way of Emmanuel. The truth of the matter is that Jesus *could not* save himself, not because of any physical constraint, but because of a moral imperative. He came to do his Father's will, and he would not be deflected from it. The One who cries in anguish in the garden of Gethsemane, "Not my will, but yours be done," is under such a divine moral imperative from his heavenly Father that disobedience is finally unthinkable. It was not nails that held Jesus to that wretched cross; it was his unqualified resolution, out of love for his Father, to do his Father's will—and, within that framework, it was his love for sinners like me. He really could not save himself. *Jesus would not save himself*

Perhaps part of our slowness to come to grips with this truth lies in the way the notion of moral imperative has dissipated in much recent Western thought. Did you see the film *Titanic* that was screened about a dozen years ago? The great ship is full of the richest people in the world, and, according to the film, as the ship sinks, the rich men start to scramble for the few and inadequate lifeboats, shoving aside the women and children in their desperate desire to live. British sailors draw handguns and fire into the air, crying "Stand back! Stand back! Women and children first!" In reality, of course, nothing like that happened. The universal testimony of the witnesses who survived the disaster is that the men hung back and urged the women and children into the lifeboats. John Jacob Astor was there, at the time the richest man on earth, the Bill Gates of 1912. He dragged his wife to a boat, shoved her on, and stepped back. Someone urged him to get in, too. He refused: the boats are too few, and must be for the women and children first. He stepped back, and drowned. The philanthropist Benjamin Guggenheim was present. He was traveling with his mistress, but when he perceived that it was unlikely he would survive, he told one of his servants, "Tell my wife that Benjamin Guggenheim knows his duty"—and he hung back, and drowned. There is not a single report of some rich man displacing women and children in the mad rush for survival.

When the film was reviewed in the *New York Times*, the reviewer asked why the producer and director of the film had distorted history so flagrantly in this regard. The scene as they depicted it was implausible from the beginning. British sailors drawing handguns? Most British police officers do not carry handguns; British sailors certainly do not. So why this willful distortion of history? And then the reviewer answered his own question: if the producer and director had told the truth, he said, no one would have believed them.

I have seldom read a more damning indictment of the development of Western culture, especially Anglo-Saxon culture, in the last century. One hundred years ago, there remained in our culture enough residue of the Christian virtue of self-sacrifice for the sake of others, of the *moral imperative* that seeks the other's good at personal expense, that Christians and non-Christians alike thought it noble, if unremarkable, to choose death for the sake of others. A mere century later, such a course is judged so unbelievable that the history has to be distorted.

So we have reached a time when a powerful internal, moral, imperative is not easily understood. Small wonder, then, that the moral imperative under which Jesus himself operated has to be explained and justified.

Moreover, Christians today will understand that biblically authentic Christianity is never merely a matter of rules and regulations, of public liturgy and private morality. Biblical Christianity results in *transformed* men and women—men and women who, because of the power of the Spirit of God, enjoy regenerated natures. We *want* to please God, we *want* to be holy, we *want* to confess Jesus is Lord. In short, because of the grace secured by Christ's cross, we ourselves experience something of a transforming moral imperative: the sins we once loved we learn to fear and hate, the obedience and holiness we once despised we now hunger for. God help us, we are woefully inconsistent in all this, but we have already tasted enough of the powers of the age to come that we know what a transforming moral imperative feels like in our lives, and we long for its perfection at the final triumph of Christ.

That is why we Christians will rejoice in this double irony: the man who can't save himself—saves others.

The Man Who Cries Out in Despair Trusts God (Matt. 27:43–51a)

Still sneering, the chief priests, teachers of the law, and elders cry mockingly, "He trusts in God. Let God rescue him now if he wants him, for he said, 'I am the Son of God'" (v. 43). Once again, their words are meant to convey sarcastic, ironic humor. When they say, "He trusts in God," what they really mean, of course, is that his trust could not have been real, it could not have been valid, for he has been abandoned by God himself. Otherwise why would he be hanging from this wretched instrument of torture?

Those crucified with him join in the abuse (v. 44). Indeed, at first reading, Jesus' cry of desolation almost seems to warrant the bitter skepticism as to whether Jesus truly trusts in God: *Eloi, Eloi, lama sabachthani?* "My God, my God, why have you forsaken me?" (v. 46). Some contemporary commentators insist that these words demonstrate that at this point Jesus does in reality abandon his trust in God. The appropriate pastoral application, they conclude, is that if even Jesus can crack when he is subjected to enough pressure, then it is not too surprising if we sometimes crack, too. We should not be too hard on ourselves, they say, if we lose our confidence in God, if we abandon trust in God, since even Jesus could lose his trust in his heavenly Father.

But this reading of the passage—we'll call it "the self-pitying Jesus" view—does not make sense of the context. First, it does not make sense of the fact that throughout these scenes, as we have seen, while the mockers think they are laughing at Jesus with witty irony, there is always a deeper irony. So here Matthew knows, and the readers know, and God knows, that Jesus *does* trust in God. The deep irony of verse 43 is that the mockers, as usual, are speaking better than they know: Jesus *does* trust his heavenly Father. But that means his cry of desolation cannot be read as evidence that he does *not* trust his heavenly Father.

Second, the cry of desolation is of course a quotation from the Davidic psalm, Psalm 22:1. But that psalm is rich in expressions of confidence and trust in God. If David can utter such an anguished cry while demonstrating his own steadfast trust in God, why should it be thought so unthinkable that David's greater Son should not utter the same cry while exercising the same trust?

Third, Jesus has just come through the agony of Gethsemane. Despite his immeasurable repugnance at the prospect of the cross, Jesus prays, "Father, if it is not possible for this cup to be taken away unless I drink it, may your will be done" (26:42). In other words, there is not a scrap of evidence that Jesus was suddenly surprised by the cross. He knew all along that this was his Father's will, and he expresses his resolution to do his Father's will.

Fourth, Jesus has already given evidence that he understands his death is for the sake of others, a ransom for sinners, a payment that effects the remission of sins, the shedding of his blood—that is, a bloody sacrifice—that seals the new covenant, a Passover sacrifice where the lamb dies, and because of that substitution the people of God do not die. Those categories are *already* established in Matthew. Jesus' cry of desolation *must* be interpreted within that framework, *not* within the framework of contemporary pop psychology that is rather keen on "the self-pitying Jesus" view.

Fifth, the narrative carefully spells out how darkness falls upon the land, and it is this darkness that precipitates Christ's anguished cry. In the light of everything that has been spelled out so far, this darkness can signal, somehow, only the absence of God, the Father's judicial frown—even though this entire sacrifice is the Father's indescribably wonderful plan—as the weight of sin and guilt crushes Jesus, who bears the penalty alone. We hover, breathless, at the edge of the mystery of the Trinity, as the Triune God's matchless love is displayed in the sacrifice of the cross, in the penal, substitutionary death of the eternal, incarnate, Son of God—Emmanuel, God with us.

Sixth, at the very moment when Jesus gives up his spirit (v. 50), Matthew reports, "The curtain of the temple was torn in two from top to bottom" (v. 51a). This is not some mere datum of interesting destruction. The destruction of the curtain makes a *theological* statement. Up to this point, the curtain signaled that only the high priest could enter into the presence of the holy God and only once a year, on the Day of Atonement—and even then the high priest, when he went behind the curtain, had to be carrying the blood of bull and goat, the animals that had been slaughtered as substitutionary deaths that averted the wrath of God and paid for the sins of the priest and the people, according to the stipulations of the old covenant. With the tearing of the temple curtain, however, the way into the presence of God is open to everyone, for the shed blood of Jesus Christ has made the perfect and final payment for sin. We no longer need mediating animal sacrifices and mediating priests; we no longer need repeated ritual. The wrath of God has been finally and forever averted from the people of the new covenant. The tearing of the curtain cries out in happy witness to the success of Christ's cross work. That means the wrath of God *has* been averted, and the cry of desolation must be interpreted as the measure of Jesus' anguish as he bears the full weight of the divine condemnation from which we are now freed.

Seventh, in exactly the same way, the miraculous temporary resurrections of verses 51 to 53 must be understood as the beginning of the death of death, the unwinding of sin and all its consequences.

So here is the fourth irony: The man who cries out in despair—trusts God.

One of the great English hymn writers was William Cowper. Cowper was a brilliant scholar who wrote distinguished critical essays for the students of Oxford and Cambridge, but in his distinctively Christian work he combined with his friend and pastor John Newton to compose and publish hymns of great depth and power. But people sometimes forget that Cowper wrestled with deep, clinical depression all his life; four times he was institutionalized for long periods in an insane asylum. Each time when he was released he was nursed back to health and strength by a kind Christian woman in the church John Newton served as pastor. About a century after Cowper's death, the great poet Elizabeth Barrett Browning wrote a three-page poem entitled, "Cowper's Grave." In it she describes the extraordinary influence of Cowper's scholarship, hymnody, and personal piety. Then she begins to allude to his horrible, dark nights of the soul. And then, powerfully referring to Jesus' cry of desolation, she writes:

> Yea, once Immanuel's orphaned cry this universe hath shaken.
> It went up single, echoless, "My God! I am forsaken!"
> It went up from the Holy's lips amidst his lost creation,
> That of the lost, no son should use these words of desolation.

Do you hear what the poet is saying? Jesus cries this agonizing cry, "My God! I am forsaken!"—so that for all eternity, William Cowper would not have to. In his depressions Cowper doubtless felt utterly abandoned, but Christ's cry ensures that for all eternity Cowper will never cry the same cry. Jesus cries this cry, "My God! I am forsaken!" so that for all eternity Don Carson will not have to. Hear the ironies of the cross:

Mary Lou

1) The man who is mocked as king—is king.
2) The man who is utterly powerless—is powerful.
3) The man who can't save himself—saves others.
4) The man who cries out in despair—trusts God.

On that wretched day the soldiers mocked him,
Raucous laughter in a barracks room,
"Hail the king!" they sneered, while spitting on him,
Brutal beatings on this day of gloom.
Though his crown was thorn, he was born a king—
Holy brilliance bathed in bleeding loss—
All the soldiers blind to this stunning theme:
Jesus reigning from a cursed cross.

Awful weakness mars the battered God-man,
Far too broken now to hoist the beam.
Soldiers strip him bare and pound the nails in,
Watch him hanging on the cruel tree.
God's own temple's down! He has been destroyed!
Death's remains are laid in rock and sod.
But the temple rises in God's wise ploy:
Our great temple is the Son of God.

"Here's the One who says he cares for others,
One who says he came to save the lost.
How can we believe that he saves others
When he can't get off that bloody cross?

Let him save himself! Let him come down now!"—
Savage jeering at the King's disgrace.
But by hanging there is precisely how
Christ saves others as the King of grace.

Draped in darkness, utterly rejected,
Crying, "Why have you forsaken me?"
Jesus bears God's wrath alone, dejected—
Weeps the bitt'rest tears instead of me.
All the mockers cry, "He has lost his trust!
He's defeated by hypocrisy!"
But with faith's resolve, Jesus knows he must
Do God's will and swallow death for me.

But now a righteousness from God, apart from law has been made known, to which the Law and the Prophets testify. This righteousness from God comes through faith in Jesus Christ to all who believe. There is no difference for all have sinned and fall short of the glory of God, and are justified freely by his grace through the redemption that came by Christ Jesus. God presented him as a sacrifice of atonement, through faith in his blood. He did this to demonstrate his justice, because in his forbearance he had left the sins committed beforehand unpunished—he did it to demonstrate his justice at the present time, so as to be just and the one who justifies those who have faith in Jesus.

—ROMANS 3:21–26

2

The Center of the
Whole Bible

Romans 3:21–26

There are some parts of the Bible that are "loose" in the sense that they are not too tight, not too condensed. They flow easily; you can readily follow the line of thought. Often they are narratives. There are other parts that are tightly reasoned; they are hard to understand and may cause your eyes to glaze over when you read right through them. You encounter so many theological words that unless you know the passage extremely well, you are reading the words, but you are not following it. It is just too much too fast. You must unpack such passages phrase by phrase if you are to gain more than vague impressions. Romans 3:21–26 is one of those passages.

After reading a text like this, what you have to do is slow down and unpack it. After you have carefully unpacked it, then you read it again—and immediately you see how it all hangs together. So if you have just read Romans 3:21–26 again and still feel that you have not grasped its flow, hang in there. By the end of this chapter, you will be able to see how what God here says through the apostle Paul hangs together. Perhaps you will also see why Martin Luther called this passage "the chief point and the very central place of the epistle to the Romans and of the whole Bible."[1]

---

[1] Margin of the Luther Bible, on Rom. 3:23ff.

Where the Passage Falls in Romans

The passage needs to be set within the framework of Romans. This paragraph is located immediately after the large block of material that runs from 1:18 to 3:20. The central point of that block is to prove, quite frankly, that we are all damned. Romans 1:18 begins the section: "The wrath of God is being revealed from heaven against all the godlessness and wickedness of human beings who suppress the truth by their wickedness." Then Paul lays out the evidence as to how we suppress the truth. Paul argues that we deny the signs of God's eternal power that are found in the creation itself. We refuse to acknowledge him as God, utterly abandon any sense of dependence and gratitude, care nothing for what brings glory to God, and end up corrupting our own thought processes. As Paul puts it, "Their thinking became futile and their foolish hearts were darkened" (1:21). Ultimately we distort even our own sexuality, our maleness and femaleness, slouching comfortably toward infidelity and perversion. Both Jews and Gentiles, Paul insists, stand under God's well-deserved curse. The Jews have not lived up to the standard of the great revelation that we now call the Old Testament (the Hebrew canon). Gentiles have not lived up to what they *do* know, whether that knowledge has come from their very constitution as human beings (after all, all of us were made in the image of God) or from socially constrained moral structures. In sum: our consciences are strong enough to condemn us because whatever revelation we have received—whether from the Bible, from nature, or from our very constitution as human beings—we do not live up to what we *do* know. We stand under the righteous wrath of God.

Paul's argument in 1:18–3:20 clashes powerfully with our culture. It ends in 3:9–18 with a list of quotations from the Old Testament designed to prove one point: all human beings are sinful. It is a terrifying passage, and it bears on one of the hardest truths to communicate today:

There is no one righteous, not even one;
>   there is no one who understands,
>   no one who seeks God.
All have turned away,
>   they have together become worthless;
there is no one who does good,
>   not even one. (Ps. 14:1–3; cf. 53:1–3; Eccl. 7:20)

Their throats are open graves;
>   their tongues practice deceit. (Ps. 5:9)

The poison of vipers is on their lips. (Ps. 140:3)

Their mouths are full of cursing and bitterness. (Ps. 10:7)

Their feet are swift to shed blood;
>   ruin and misery mark their ways,
and the way of peace they do not know. (Isa. 59:7–8)

There is no fear of God before their eyes. (Ps. 36:1)

When I do university missions today, for the most part I am speaking to biblical illiterates. The hardest truth to get across to them is not the existence of God, the Trinity, the deity of Christ, Jesus' substitutionary atonement, or Jesus' resurrection. Even if they think these notions are a bit silly, they are likely to respond, "Oh, so that's what Christians believe." They can see a certain coherence to these notions. No, the hardest truth to get across to this generation is what the Bible says about sin.

Sin is generally a snicker-word: you say it, and everybody snickers. There is no shame attached to it. It is so hard to get across how ugly sin is to God. When I talk about sin, I have "gone to meddling." I am not talking about a group of external ideas that people may or may not believe;

I am talking about a category they feel they must repudiate. There is so much in our culture that teaches us that we define our own sins, either individually or socially (i.e., we belong to a certain community that has established its own heritage of rights and wrongs). For somebody else to come in and say, "This is right" or "That's wrong" sounds like manipulation from the outside, and they think that it fails to recognize the social origins of all constructions of good and evil. They sometimes become so indignant with this notion of sin that I must spend a lot of time talking about it!

We live in an age where the one wrong thing to say is that somebody else is wrong. One of the impacts of postmodern epistemology is that we all have our own independent points of view, and we look at things from the perspective of our own small interpretive communities. What is sin to one group is not sin to another group. But not only does the Bible insist that there is such a thing as sin, it insists that the heart of its ugly offensiveness is its horrible odiousness to God—how it offends God. Thus, Romans 1:18 begins not with analyzing sin from a social perspective but by observing God's response to it: "The wrath of God is being revealed from heaven against all the godlessness and wickedness of men who suppress the truth by their wickedness." Then chapter 2 shows that religion by itself does not help, and chapter 3 concludes that Jews and Gentiles alike are all under wrath. All of this is climaxed by the list of quotations I've just cited from 3:9–18. Even though this is very hard to absorb in our culture, I cannot too strongly insist that unless this stance is understood, our passage, Romans 3:21–26, will make very little sense because we will not grasp the nature of the problem being addressed.

Some of us have a view of the gospel that makes Jesus out to be something like an automobile club repairman: Jesus is a nice man, he's a very, very nice man, and when you break down, he comes along and fixes you. Yet what Paul depicts here is that the nature of our brokenness turns first and foremost on our offensiveness to God. It is the wrath of God that is disclosed from heaven. Paul is certainly not denying that there are many kinds of social parameters to sin; he is not overlooking the raw fact that sinners can also be victims. Perpetrators have very often been the abused. Sin is a social thing. We commit sin, and we affect others. On the other hand, if we think of ourselves only in terms of victimhood, then we need only a healer or repairer. If all the damage we do is exclusively horizontal, what we need *most* is social transformation. Of course, the Bible can picture God and his salvation in these sorts of categories. Yet in the Bible the most fundamental category of all to which the biblical writers resort in order to portray the nature of the problem is our offensiveness before God. It follows that what is needed first and foremost for us to be saved—for this situation to change—is to provide a means by which we may be reconciled to this God.

As a rule, unless people agree on what the problem is, they cannot agree on what the solution is. Unless we can agree on what we are being saved from, we cannot agree on what salvation itself is. For example, if we decide that the fundamental human problem is simply our location, our sense of loneliness in the universe, our sense of inadequacy, or our pathetic levels of self-esteem, we will tilt the gospel to meet this perceived need. "Don't you realize that the gospel will give you your needed sense of self-importance? That will solve the problem of self-esteem." "Don't you recognize that the fundamental human problem is economic injustice? The good news is that God is all for justice. Preach this gospel and our cultures will be transformed." I hasten to add that the Bible does dare to address matters of how we are to think of ourselves—matters that therefore bear on self-esteem—and it is concerned with justice. Yet on the face of it Paul is convinced that the root problem is our rebellion against God, our fascination with idolatry, our grotesque de-godding of God.

Some might reply, "Haven't you ever heard of wonderful organizations like 'Doctors Without Borders'? Don't you believe in the notion of common grace? We do so much good in the world." Paul does not deny any of that. Cornelius, prior to becoming a Christian, was thought of as a good man in relative terms.

Yet in the absolute sense of measuring up to God's standards, this is what Paul says. And the interesting thing about this long list of references is that they are all from the Old Testament. Paul quotes the Bible to underscore that this is what God says about this situation.

Even when we are doing the good—whatever it is that we do—it is still so habitually done independently of God because we are going to be our own gods. We are at the center of the universe. Thus, we end up de-godding God in order to be able to sing with Frank Sinatra, "I did it *my* way." This is the very heart of all idolatry. All the bad stuff that sluices down the corridors of history emerges finally through that vaunted, awful self-independence. The fundamental problem is the universal idolatry of humans: we de-god God.

Even when we understand that this is Paul's argument in Romans 1:18–3:20, for many of us it is still difficult to feel empathy with Paul's stance as he provides his list of Old Testament quotations in 3:9–20. They seem a bit over the top, almost a grotesque negativism. After all, you do not go around saying, "I'm at the center of the universe."

On the other hand, if someone were suddenly to hold up a picture of your graduating class from high school or college and say, "This is your graduating class," which face do you look for first—just to make sure it is there?

Or if you have an argument—a real humdinger, a knock-downdrag-'em-out-one-in-ten-years argument, a real first-class roustabout argument—and you go away just seething, thinking of all the things that you could have said, all the things you should have said, all the things you would have said if you had thought of them fast enough, and then you replay the whole argument in your mind—who wins?

I have lost a lot of arguments in my time, but I have never lost a mental rerun.

The problem is that if I think that I am at the center of the universe, then most likely you do, too. And frankly, you stupid twit, how dare you set yourself up over against me? And now, instead of God being at the center, each human being, each of God's own image bearers, thinks he or she is at the center. We find our self-identity *not* in being God's creature, but in any other person, institution, value system, ritual—anything so that God cannot be heard, cannot be allowed to make his ultimate claim as our Creator and Judge. "God [we say]—if he or she or it exists—jolly well better serve *me*, or else, quite frankly, I will find another God." That is the beginning of idolatry.

"I'm looking for the kind of God I can believe in," you say. But this stance is both tragic and foolish, is it not? For it presupposes that the "I" is the ultimate criterion, the ultimate god. Surely the real question is, "What kind of God is there?" Otherwise you are simply manufacturing your own god, and that is what idolatry is.

Scarcely less horrific, this stance means that I am now also in conflict with all these other people who want to be at the center of the universe, and there is the beginning of war, hate, rape, and fences—all because I say, "I will be god."

God finds this deeply, profoundly, personally offensive. It is not merely tragic for us since we are destroying ourselves; it is also abominably disgusting to God. It is degrading to God. That is why the Old

Testament connects God's wrath with idolatry. That is also why in the New Testament covetousness can be talked about in terms of idolatry. If you want something badly enough, that thing becomes god for you. It is idolatry, which means that instead of wanting God, you want the thing, which de-gods God. That is why Jesus says that the first commandment is to love God with all your heart and soul and mind and strength. This is the one commandment that you break when you break any other commandment. Whenever we sin, this is the reason why, regardless of the sin, the most offended person is God.

Not too long ago I read a piece called "Escape from Nihilism" by J. Budziszewski (pronounced boo-jee-SHEF-ski). Before he became a Christian, Budziszewski earned his PhD in ethics, forcefully arguing that we make our own rules for right and wrong, establishing our own moral structures. At the time, he was an atheistic philosopher of religion who taught at the University of Texas. After he abandoned his atheism, he reflected on his shift:

> I have already noted in passing that everything goes wrong without God. This is true even of the good things he has given us, such as our minds. One of the good things I've been given is a stronger than average mind. I don't make the observation to boast; human beings are given diverse gifts to serve him in diverse ways. The problem is that a strong mind that refuses the call to serve God has its own way of going wrong. When some people flee from God they rob and kill. When others flee from God they do a lot of drugs and have a lot of sex. When I fled from God I didn't do any of those things; my way of fleeing was to get stupid. Though it always comes as a surprise to intellectuals, there are some forms of stupidity that one must be highly intelligent and educated to achieve. God keeps them in his arsenal to pull down mulish pride, and I discovered them all. That is how I ended up doing a doctoral dissertation to prove that we make up the difference between

good and evil and that we aren't responsible for what we do. I remember now that I even taught these things to students. Now that's sin.

It was also agony. You cannot imagine what a person has to do to himself—well, if you are like I was, maybe you can—what a person has to do to himself to go on believing such nonsense. St. Paul said that the knowledge of God's law is "written on our hearts, our consciences also bearing witness." The way natural law thinkers put this is to say that they constitute the deep structure of our minds. That means that so long as we have minds, we can't *not* know them. Well, I was unusually determined not to know them; therefore I had to destroy my mind. I resisted the temptation to believe in good with as much energy as some saints resist the temptation to neglect good. For instance, I loved my wife and children, but I was determined to regard this love as merely a subjective preference with no real and objective value. Think what this did to my very capacity to love them. After all, love is a commitment of the will to the true good of another person, and how can one's will be committed to the true good of another person if he denies the reality of good, denies the reality of persons, and denies that his commitments are in his control?

Visualize a man opening up the access panels of his mind and pulling out all the components that have God's image stamped on them. The problem is that they all have God's image stamped on them, so the man can never stop. No matter how many he pulls out, there are still more to pull. I was that man. Because I pulled out more and more, there was less and less that I could think about. But because there was less and less that I could think about, I thought I was becoming more and more focused. Because I believed things that filled me with dread, I thought I was smarter and braver than the people who didn't believe them. I thought I saw an emptiness at the heart of the universe that was hidden from their foolish eyes. But I was the fool.[2]

Then he describes how grace began to call him and recounts steps to his belief in God. Here is a man who is beginning to understand Romans 1:18–3:20.

---

[2]In *re:generation Quarterly* 4/1 (1998): 12–15.

I have a friend in Australia who often does university missions, and he occasionally preaches a message entitled "Atheists Are Fools, and Agnostics Are Cowards." Now, I am not suggesting that this is a title all of us should choose. He is an Aussie, and Aussies tend to be a little more direct than most of the rest of us. But at a certain level, it is easy to sympathize with what he is saying. From God's perspective, it is the fool who has said in his heart, "There is no God" (Ps. 14:1).

The point is that unless you really see the lostness of us human beings in our rebellion against God, it is very difficult to make sense of what comes next.

What Paul Establishes in Romans 3:21–26

In the passage in front of us, Paul talks about the solution, how we are to be just before God. The controlling expression in this paragraph is "the righteousness of God." The expression, which could be rendered "the justice of God" or "the justification of God," occurs four times in these six verses. The verb *to justify* occurs an additional two times, and the adjective *just* or *righteous* occurs once. This whole passage has to do with how a person can be considered just before this holy God, granted that our condition is as miserable as it is made out to be in the first two and a half chapters. To get at the heart of Paul's solution, we will reflect on the four steps that he establishes in his argument.

1) Paul establishes the relationship of God's righteousness in Christ to the Old Testament's law covenant (3:21).

"But now" introduces something new into Paul's argument. This is not just a logical transition: "but now, at this step in the argument . . ." Paul can use "but now" in diverse ways, but in this context the expression means, "*But now*, at this point in the stream of redemptive history." Something new has come along.

What is the nature of the change that Paul here envisages? In the past there was something else, "but now" what is there?

A popular but misguided view is that in the Old Testament God was especially wrathful, "but now" in the New Testament God is especially loving and gracious. The argument runs like this: in the old covenant, God demonstrated himself in righteous wrath, not least in famines, plagues, and war. Now, however, under the terms of the new covenant established by the cross, God displays a gentler side to his character in the gospel. Many Christians think that in the Old Testament God is almost bad-tempered, while in the New Testament Jesus tells his followers to turn the other cheek—and he himself goes to the cross on our behalf. So when Paul introduces his paragraph with the words "but now," he is preparing to paint a portrait of God that is a little softer than what is found in the Old Testament.

For at least three reasons, this view is a huge mistake. First, while there is plenty of judgment in the Old Testament, those same Old Testament documents affirm, with equal fervor, God's kindness, generosity, love, and grace. For instance:

> The LORD is compassionate and gracious,
>   slow to anger, abounding in love.[3]
> He will not always accuse,
>   nor will he harbor his anger forever. . . .
> As a father has compassion on his children,
>   so the LORD has compassion on those who fear him;
> for he knows how we are formed,
>   he remembers that we are dust. (Ps. 103:8–9, 13–14)

There are many, many passages of that sort. The psalmists are constantly praising God for his mercy, patience, forbearance, and so forth. The Old

---

[3]Cf. Ex. 34:6; Num. 14:18; Neh. 9:17; Pss. 86:15; 103:8; 145:8; Joel 2:13; Jonah 4:2; Nah. 1:3.

Testament does not picture God as some bad-tempered, short-fused boor who is anxious to say, "Zap! Gotcha!"

Second, this view does not adequately account for the New Testament's depiction of God's wrath. It is not as if once we turn to the New Testament all the clouds suddenly lift. Yes, there are some wonderful descriptions of God and his love, and Jesus does teach us to turn the other cheek. But almost all of the most colorful metaphorical depictions of hell come from Jesus—not exactly "gentle Jesus, meek and mild." Before one decides that the God of the New Testament is displayed exclusively in terms of sweetness, kindness, and light, it is worth remembering passages such as Revelation 14:17–20:

> Another angel came out of the temple in heaven, and he too had a sharp sickle. Still another angel, who had charge of the fire, came from the altar and called in a loud voice to him who had the sharp sickle, "Take your sharp sickle and gather the clusters of grapes from the earth's vine, because its grapes are ripe." The angel swung his sickle on the earth, gathered its grapes and threw them into the great winepress of God's wrath. They were trampled in the winepress outside the city, and blood flowed out of the press, rising as high as the horses' bridles for a distance of 1,600 stadia.

This imagery—and it is imagery—is drawn from ancient wine vats, stone vats into which one threw ripe grapes. The servant girls would then kick off their sandals, pull up their skirts, and trample down the grapes. At the bottom of the vats were little holes with channels under them, and the grape juice would get squeezed out of the grapes to run off to be collected in bottles. In this adaptation of such imagery, *people* are being thrown into this winepress of God's wrath, and they are being trampled down until their blood flows to a distance of 200 miles at the height of a horse's bridle. Now, you tell me that the picture of God in the New Testament is of a softer, gentler, kinder God.

I suspect that the reason we even think like that—even for a moment—is that in the Old Testament the pictures of God's wrath are temporal, expressed primarily in historical terms. In the New Testament the pictures of God's wrath are primarily (though not exclusively) in final eschatological and apocalyptic terms—and most of us do not really believe the latter, so we are not frightened of them. Our culture is so present-oriented that we filter out depictions of final judgment; we are not frightened of hell. We are far more frightened of war, old age, sickness, disease, and bankruptcy. We are more frightened of temporal judgments than final judgment. We skirt through the pictures of judgment in the New Testament, with the result that they do not bother us much. But when it comes to plague, pestilence, and war, then we are scared witless. That says much about our focus on this present life.

The move from the Old Testament to the New Testament is not a move from a wrathful God to a loving God. Rather, the New Testament ratchets up both themes. The depictions of both God's wrath and God's love are ratcheted up in intensity in the New Testament documents. The cross spectacularly displays God's love, but it also displays God's wrath against sin; it massively underscores God's condemnation of sin.

Third, this view does not make adequate sense of the rest of Romans 3:21. In a nutshell, Paul's argument in this verse is this: in redemptive history God's people prior to the cross were under the Mosaic law covenant, "but now" God's righteousness has been made known apart from that law covenant.

The prepositional phrase "apart from the law" can be translated in at least two ways. It modifies either "the righteousness of God" or "has been made known."

1) "But now *a righteousness from God apart from law* has been made known." On this reading, the righteousness from God is itself apart from

law (e.g., apart from keeping the law). This view misses the point of the passage.

2) "But now *apart from law* the righteousness of God has been made known." It is not a different righteousness; rather, the righteousness of God "has been made known" in a different way, namely, apart from the law covenant. From Moses on, all the demonstration of God's righteousness in the Old Testament is bound up with the structure of the Mosaic covenant. That was the covenant under which God's people found themselves. "But now" we have come to the end of the law covenant. Paul introduces a new covenant, which Jeremiah pointed to six hundred years before Christ (Jer. 31:31ff.). The Old Testament anticipated a priest-king in the order of Melchizedek, not simply a priest in the order of Levi bound up with the Mosaic covenant (Ps. 110). So now this righteousness from God is here, and we need it to solve the problem of the first two and a half chapters to be just before God. This display of God's righteousness has been revealed apart from the law covenant.

Before telling us exactly how this works, however, Paul hastens to insist that even if this righteousness from God has been disclosed apart from law, he does not want people to think that the righteousness from God has nothing to do with the law covenant or that the new covenant is so completely cut off from the Old Testament that quite frankly we can now scrap the Old Testament. Paul immediately adds another clause: the righteousness from God of which he is speaking is that "to which the Law and the Prophets testify." Paul insists that if you rightly read the Old Testament, you will discover that these very writings, rightly understood, point forward to, testify to, anticipate, and prophesy what has culminated in Christ. Yes, we are under a new covenant, but the old covenant anticipated what now is. The new covenant is the fulfillment of the old covenant.

Reading the Old Testament in this way should not be surprising to

Christians. After all, we do something similar when we read the initial Old Testament Passover account. The angel of death passed over the land of Egypt, and all those who were in homes protected by the blood of a lamb sprinkled on the doorposts and lintel were saved from wrath: the angel of death "passed over" them. Paul then writes, "Christ, our Passover lamb, has been sacrificed" (1 Cor. 5:7). By his death, we have been saved from well-deserved wrath: Christ was sacrificed for us, and wrath has "passed over" us. In short, there are good reasons for thinking that Old Testament structures are themselves looking forward to something. They are announcing something beyond themselves.

Another Old Testament example is Yom Kippur (the Day of Atonement). The letter to the Hebrews works this out in great detail. In the Old Testament the priest took the blood of a bull and a goat and went in to the Holy of Holies, the most holy place, the cube-shaped room in the tabernacle, and sprinkled on the top of the ark of the covenant the blood of the animals, both for his own sins and for the sins of the people. But the ultimate sacrifice, the ultimate payment for sins, is surely not the blood of a bull or a goat. How could such blood pay for anything in a final way? The writer to the Hebrews lines up his arguments to show that such blood finally points forward to the blood of Christ himself (see esp. Hebrews 9–10).

So also in the passage before us. Under the terms of the old covenant, it was impossible to think of God's righteousness apart from the many strictures of that Old Testament covenant. "But now" a righteousness has been revealed *apart* from that covenant—even though, Paul insists, the law and the prophets bore anticipatory witness to what Jesus is putting in place under the terms of the new covenant. Paul establishes the revelation of God's righteousness in its relation to the Old Testament; he sets forth the roots of the good news in the pages of the Old Testament.

2) *Paul establishes the availability of God's righteousness for all human beings, without ethnic distinction but on condition of faith (3:22–23).*

Verse 22 says, "This righteousness [i.e., the righteousness described in 3:21] from God comes through *faith* in Jesus Christ to all who *believe*." In English, the noun *faith* sounds different from the verb *believe*. The two English words come from two separate roots. But in Greek these words share the same root: *pist-* (*faith* is *pistis* and *to believe* is *pisteuō*). Here is a rendering that uses English words to show you how they sound the same in Greek: "This righteousness from God comes through *trust* in Jesus Christ to all who *trust*." The word *trust* can function as both a noun and a verb. But that translation, like the Greek, sounds a bit repetitious.

Partly because of that repetition, people have sometimes taken the first word, "faith," to mean what it sometimes means elsewhere: not "faith" (or "trust"), but "faithfulness." They read it this way: "This righteousness from God comes through the *faithfulness* [or trustworthiness] of Jesus Christ to all who *believe*." This gets rid of the repetition: the first occurrence refers to *Jesus'* faithfulness, and the second to *our* faith. Moreover, this rendering makes theological sense. It still maintains an emphasis on faith ("to all who *believe*"), but it "comes through the faithfulness of Jesus Christ." The New Testament (particularly John's Gospel and Hebrews) certainly emphasizes Jesus' faithfulness: he obeys his Father; he is faithful to the very end; he is faithful over the whole house where God has made him the Son. In short, this alternative rendering makes a certain kind of theological sense. Yet it really isn't what the text means. Throughout Romans 3 and 4, Paul repeatedly returns to the notion of "faith," and in every single case he is referring to *our faith*, not to *Jesus' faithfulness*.[4]

---

[4]The finest linguistic treatment of the "faith of Christ" debate ("faith in Christ" vs. "faithfulness of Christ") is by Moisés Silva, "Faith Versus Works of Law in Galatians," in *Justification and Variegated Nomism: The Paradoxes of Paul*, ed. D. A. Carson, Peter T. O'Brien, and Mark A. Seifrid, WUNT 181 (Grand Rapids: Baker, 2004), 217–48.

That raises the question, "Why then does Paul repeat himself?" If this is talking about our faith in Jesus, why does he repeat it ("to all who *believe*")? The reason is bound up with the little word "all": "This righteousness from God comes through faith in Jesus Christ to *all* who believe [*because*] there is no difference, for all have sinned and fall short of the glory of God." The reason for the repetition is to emphasize "all," which connects this paragraph with 1:18–3:20: *all* are under sin, *all* are condemned, and *all* need God's righteousness. To paraphrase it again: "This righteousness from God comes through faith in Jesus Christ to *all* who have faith. For *there is no difference* between Jew and Gentile, for *all* sin and fall short of the glory of God." To fall short of the glory of God, to fall short of giving him the glory that he deserves, lies at the center of the idolatry the entire Bible condemns, and all of us are guilty, as the apostle has just taken almost three chapters to demonstrate.

In other words Paul spends two and a half chapters showing that all human beings sin, and the only way that this "righteousness from God" that is now appearing can address the sweep of that universal need is if it is available in principle to all without ethnic distinction: Jew and Gentile alike. Jew and Gentile are both condemned and both savable. This righteousness from God is available not simply to Jews under the terms of the old covenant or to those who become Jews by taking on the restrictions of the old covenant (e.g., being circumcised); it comes to *all* who have faith. It is open in principle to all human beings without ethnic distinction but on condition of faith. That is part of what makes this new covenant *new*.

The old Mosaic covenant was bound up with a certain ethnic group, the Israelites. If you wanted to participate in the blessings of that covenant, it was not enough just to go and live in Israel. To become a legal Israelite, sooner or later you had to come under the terms of the covenant. The blessings of the covenant were mediated through the terms of that covenant. We might paraphrase: "But now a righteousness from God has appeared apart from that law covenant, although that law covenant testifies to this. And this righteousness from God comes through trust in Jesus Christ—to *all* who trust in Jesus Christ. For there is no difference between Jew and Gentile, for all sin and fall short of the glory of God." That is precisely what ties this paragraph to the previous two and a half chapters. The solution meets the need. There is not a whiff of racism here. We are all guilty before God, and the cross is our only hope.

If we are Christians, we are used to this sweep of things, this vision of the grace of God that crosses all ethnicities. Nevertheless, the wonder of it needs to fall on us again. Around the throne on the last day, there will be many men and women from every tongue and tribe and people and nation—not just white, middle-class Americans (see Revelation 4–5). This spectacular diversity is something that wonderfully emphasizes the unity. See, for example, Ephesians 2, where Jew and Gentile are brought together into one new humanity in Christ Jesus because we have been saved by grace alone through faith alone in order to produce the good works that God has ordained from before the foundation of the world.

This is similar to the end of Galatians 3. As far as our standing before God is concerned, if this gospel is true, then in Christ there is neither Jew nor Greek, slave nor free, male nor female. This is an incredibly sweeping breadth, for this righteousness from God is open to those who have faith in Christ—to *all* who have faith in Christ, for *all* are lost and fall under sin's condemnation and desperately need the forgiveness that only God himself provides.

All people without distinction are both condemned and savable: Jew and Gentile alike, Jews and Arabs alike, blacks and whites alike,

Westerners and Easterners alike, Northerners and Southerners alike. Pragmatically, this needs to be worked out. Of course, there are some churches that are situated in neighborhoods that draw from only one ethnic group. In that case the way you demonstrate the truth of this passage may be by linking up with churches that are grounded in other ethnicities. Mix and match and swap ministers for a week or two—something to demonstrate that you are not simply *American* Christians but that you are *Christian* Christians. But if your church is in a neighborhood where the population is already diverse, ideally one of the things you should want to do, you should be *trying* to do, is demonstrate that community diversity in your congregation: a community of believers who are different but nevertheless have an incredible oneness and unity in Christ Jesus.

I suspect that if I were not a Christian, I would not spend a lot of time seeking out people who are very different from me. I like people who are like me. But if this gospel is important to me and important to you, then we will discover that we have links with the strangest people all over the world. Part of my job takes me to country after country. I have come to know brothers and sisters in Christ in many dozens of different ethnicities. This gospel, this righteousness from God, is for those who trust Christ—for *all* who trust Christ, for *all* have sinned and come short of the glory of God. Those deep commonalities must transcend our personal tastes in music, food, clothing style, economic status, sense of humor, intellectual interest, diverse national histories, and the like. Equally, it must drive our evangelism. Does not Jesus himself teach in the Sermon on the Mount that any pagan can find friends among people who are like him, but it takes the grace of God to transcend those kinds of limitations?

3) Paul establishes the source of God's righteousness in the gracious provision of Christ Jesus as the propitiation for our sins (3:24–25a).

Two terms in these verses need just a wee bit of unpacking.

Redemption

In our world a word like *redemption* belongs to God-talk. In other words you normally do not talk fluently about redemption in everyday life. Redemption is something religious people talk about. Until fairly recent times, however—and still in some sectors—redemption was frequently used in an economic sense. For instance, you might redeem a mortgage. People do not speak of "redemption money" anymore, but they did a bare fifty or sixty years ago, when there were a lot more pawn shops around. If you needed some money in the great depression, you might hawk a watch. You would sell it to the pawn shop. They would keep it for three weeks or six months or whatever agreed time period before they would sell it, and in that time you could go back and redeem it; that is, you could pay money to have it freed (the amount for which you sold it plus a percentage)—to have it released so that you could have it back again. You could redeem your watch.

In the ancient world, redemption language was common. Of course, it is found in Scripture (e.g., God redeems Israel from slavery), but it was common economic language in the Greco-Roman world. It was a word commonly used on the streets in any imperial city. It was used, for example, for the redemption of slaves. In the ancient world you might become a slave as a result of losing a war or because marauding parties attacked your territory and captured you and your family. But sometimes in the ancient world you became a slave because of economic circumstances. There were no bankruptcy laws to protect you—no chapter eleven or chapter thirteen (to use categories that are familiar to Americans). So suppose you borrow some money to start a business, and you lose your shirt during an economic downturn. What do you do? You sell yourself and maybe your whole family into slavery. There is nothing else you can do. So many people became slaves in the ancient world as a result of bankruptcy.

But suppose that you have a well-to-do cousin twenty-five miles away (a day's journey) who hears that you have sold yourself into slavery. Not only is this cousin well-to-do; he is pretty decent. So he decides to buy you back. He redeems you. He travels a day's journey to where you have become a slave, and he makes an arrangement with your owner. There was adequate provision for this under the law. The way it normally worked was like this: the redeemer paid the price money for the slave to a pagan temple plus a small cut for the temple priests (and how small a cut was variable!). Then the temple paid the price money to the owner of the slave, and the slave was then transferred to the ownership of this temple's god. Thus, the slave was redeemed from the slavery to the slave owner, in order to become a slave to the god. Of course, if you are a slave to a pagan god, that basically means that you are free and can do anything you want. It was in part a legal fiction in order to say that the person does not lose his slave status but nevertheless is freed from slavery in the human sphere because the price has been paid. The man has now been redeemed.

Paul picks up that language and says that Christians have been redeemed from slavery to sin, but as a result of this, they have become slaves of Jesus Christ (see Romans 6). Many of our English translations say "*servant* of Jesus Christ," but the word most commonly used is *doulos*, which always refers to a slave. We are *slaves* of Jesus Christ. We have been redeemed from slavery to sin. Somebody has paid the price. We sing it: we have been "redeemed by the blood of the Lamb."

We are justified freely by grace, Paul writes, "through the *redemption*

that came by Christ Jesus" (3:24). The slave cannot buy his own freedom; otherwise he would not be a slave. He cannot save himself!

Now, how does this work? Paul has still not explained it. It is not literal
redemption purchased with money, and whatever it is that is paid is not
literally paid to sin. In what sense, then, are we redeemed? What has freed
us? How does it work? The answer: God presented Christ as a propitiation.

Propitiation

Translations variously say "propitiation," "expiation," "sacrifice of atonement," and even "remedy for defilement." The best translation is "propitiation." Of course, "propitiation" has to be explained. On the other
hand, all of the terms have to be explained. "Sacrifice of atonement" is
not patently obvious. If you must explain all available terms, you might
as well explain the one that is closest to the original! In this case the best
one is "propitiation." But what does it mean?

The question is particularly important because much of Paul's
argument in this paragraph turns on it. Propitiation is the act by which
someone (in this case, God) becomes propitious, that is, favorable.
Propitiation is the sacrificial act by which someone becomes favorable.

In ancient paganism, propitiation worked like this. There were a
lot of gods with various domains (god of the sea, god/goddess of fertil-
ity, god of speech, god of war, etc.) who were a bit whimsical and bad-
tempered. Your job was to make them propitious (i.e., favorable) toward
you. For example, if you wanted to take a sea voyage, you would make
sure that the god of the sea, Neptune, was favorable by offering him a
propitiating sacrifice in the hope that he would provide you with safe
passage. So the object of the propitiating sacrifice is the god himself, and
the purpose is to make the god propitious.

Expiation, by contrast, aims to cancel sin. Expiation is the sacrificial
act by which sin is canceled, removed, "expiated." The object of expia-

tion is sin. By contrast, the object of propitiation, as we've seen, is God. Expiation refers to cancelling sin, and propitiation refers to satisfying or setting aside God's wrath. The particular word used in Romans 3:25 is used most commonly in the Old Testament to refer to a propitiating sacrifice that turns aside God's wrath.

In the 1930s, C. H. Dodd, a Welsh professor, wrote an essay that had a worldwide (disruptive) impact. He made a profession of faith during the Welsh revival in 1904–1905. By the 1930s he had become quite a liberal (but pious) theologian at the University of Manchester in Britain and later taught New Testament at the University of Cambridge. In his influential essay, he argued that this word in Romans 3:25 cannot possibly mean "propitiation" because in the pagan world humans offer propitiatory sacrifices to whimsical, bad-tempered gods, but according to the Bible, God is already so propitious and loving that he sent his Son (cf. John 3:16). If God is already so favorable to us that he gives his Son, how can one speak of the Son's sacrifice on the cross as making God favorable? God is already favorable or else he would not have sent his Son in the first place. So how can Jesus' death on the cross possibly be propitiation? How much more propitious can God become than giving us his Son in the first place?

Dodd insisted that the word must really mean "expiation" (cancel-ing sin), not "propitiation," since God does not need to be made more favorable to us than he already is. Dodd's view became quite popular in the Western world. When he later edited the translation of the New English Bible, he so much hated the term *propitiation* (and did not really like the term *expiation* either) that he used the expression "remedy for defilement." While on the senior committee that was discussing the translation of Romans 3, he was overheard to mutter under his breath, "What rubbish!" In light of this, someone wrote a limerick:

There was a professor called Dodd
Whose name was exceedingly odd.
   He spelled, if you please,
   His name with three Ds,
While one is sufficient for God.

Now, that riposte does not answer a single thing, but it is a peculiarly English way of handling theological controversy! It does not get anywhere near the heart of the issue, but it is clever.

Somebody eventually pointed out to Dodd that the previous two and a half chapters of Romans are headed up by 1:18, which states that there is some sense in which God's wrath *is* against us. Dodd denied that this is real wrath but rather a metaphorical way of talking about the inevitability of moral consequences: if you do bad things, bad things will happen to you. Dodd denied that God's wrath was actually personal.[5]

I am not sure we are reading the same Bible! When you read through the Bible, whatever else the wrath of God is, it is intensely personal. "I, the LORD your God, am a jealous God, punishing the children for the sin of the fathers to the third and fourth generation of those who hate me" (Ex. 20:5). The real danger of Dodd's analysis is that God does not have much invested in all of this. There is some sort of impersonal moral law in the universe, and God is merely presiding over things from a distance. If you do something bad, inevitably bad stuff happens to you. Watch out for bad karma! God's job is to come along and save you from bad karma. But that is not the God of the Bible! Every single sin that we commit is not simply transgression of some abstract moral code so that karma takes its toll. Sin in the Bible is first and foremost offense against God. Of course, the sin must be cancelled; that is expiation. But the God who has

---

[5]For refutations of C. H. Dodd's view of propitiation, see Roger Nicole, "C. H. Dodd and the Doctrine of Propitiation," *Westminster Theological Journal* 17 (1954–1955): 117–57; and Leon Morris, *The Apostolic Preaching of the Cross*, 3rd ed. (Grand Rapids: Eerdmans, 1965).

been offended must be satisfied; that is propitiation. It is also true that in the Bible expiation and propitiation hang together: it is difficult to see how you can have one without the other (which is why some translations prefer a global expression like "sacrifice of atonement"). But we cannot ever lose sight of the fact that God is personally offended by our anarchic rebellion and is judicially angry with us.

For example, David commits adultery and then murder. When the prophet Nathan confronts David, he repents and subsequently addresses God in a psalm in which he writes, "Against you, you only, have I sinned and done what is evil in your sight" (Ps. 51:4). In one sense, of course, that was a lot of bunkum, pure hogwash. He certainly sinned against Bathsheba (he seduced her and committed adultery with her); he sinned against her husband, Uriah the Hittite (he had him bumped off); he sinned against the baby in Bathsheba's womb (the baby died, but even if the child had lived he would have been a bastard, never knowing the man who was his mother's husband); he sinned against the military high command (he corrupted them in order to have Uriah bumped off); he sinned against his own family (he betrayed them); he sinned against the whole covenant people (he betrayed the nation as their chief officer). There is nobody that he has *not* sinned against, and now he has the cheek to say, "Against you, you only, have I sinned and done what is evil in your sight" (Ps. 51:4). This makes you want to say, "David, get realistic here!" And yet there is another sense in which he is profoundly right. This is exactly the case, for what makes sin so sinful, awful, condemning, and damnably heinous is not all of its social ramifications. It is that sin is first and foremost sin against an almighty and holy God.

That is why Jesus says that the first commandment is to love God with heart and soul and mind and strength. It is the first commandment because it is the one we always break when we break anything else. Always.

It is awful. If you cheat on your income tax, the party most offended is God. If you cheat on your spouse, the party most offended is God. If you indulge in racism, the party most offended is God. If you nurture bitterness, the party most offended is God. That is what makes sin *sin*, and we must be reconciled to this God. We certainly need to have horizontal relationships restored as well, but if you have the horizontal relationships restored but do not have forgiveness from God, you do not have much! In eternal terms what you must have is God looking at you favorably.

The Bible pictures God's standing over against us in both wrath and love. That is what Dodd failed to see. An imperfect analogy is that parents can be ticked at their children at times while still loving them. God stands over against us in wrath because of our sin and his holiness. If he did not stand over against us in wrath when his holiness sees our sin, it would not say much for his holiness. "Oh, you can be a Hitler and bump off millions of people. I'm not bothered. No skin off my nose." Would that be more loving of God? Would that not contradict his holiness? Would it be more loving of God if he said to his image bearers who de-god him and relativize him, "Oh, no offense taken. I don't really care"? No, he stands over against us in wrath. God's wrath is the inevitable confrontation of God's holiness over against our sin. The remarkable thing is that God stands over against us in love just the same—not because we are so lovable or cute but because he is that kind of God. "But when the time had fully come, God sent his Son" (Gal. 4:4) to be the propitiation for our sins.

This marks the fundamental difference between pagan propitiation and Christian propitiation. In pagan propitiation, *a human being* offers a propitiatory sacrifice to make a god propitious. In Christian propitiation, *God the Father* sets forth Jesus as the propitiation to make *himself* propitious; God is both the subject and the object of propitiation. God is the one who provides the sacrifice precisely as a way of turning aside his own wrath. God the Father is thus the propitia*tor* and the propitiat*ed*, and God the Son is the propitia*tion*.

Have you ever used the following illustration to explain the gospel? God in the gospel, we sometimes say, is like a judge who has a guilty party before him at the bar, and he pronounces the sentence—whether it is five years in jail, a $10,000 fine, or whatever. Then the judge steps down from the bench, takes off his robes, and takes the person's place in prison or writes out the check for the fine. And we say, "This is what the Christian gospel is all about. It is a substitution."

I have used this or similar illustrations myself. But I do not do so anymore, for I have come to see that in itself the illustration is misleading. It is not entirely wrong, of course. It does explain something of penal substitution: another takes my place and bears my penalty. But the illustration is misleading because there is one part of it that is fundamentally skewed. In our world it cannot easily be made to align with justice. In Western judicial systems, the judge is supposed to be a neutral arbitrator or administrator of a system of law that is bigger than he or she is. The offense is not against the judge. If the judge is the one who got mugged, then when the mugger stands before him, the judge must recuse himself from the case because he is not supposed to be the offended party. That is why we speak of criminals committing an offense against the state or the law or the republic or the crown. We do not speak of an offense against the judge because if the offense is against the judge, the judge must recuse herself in order to preserve a certain kind of neutrality. If in our system a judge pronounced sentence and then went down and took the criminal's place, it would be a miscarriage of justice. The guilty person must pay. The judge does not have the right to set aside the law like that. Judges are supposed to be independent arbitrators of the system. The offense is not against them.

Let me put it another way. Suppose, God forbid, that you were attacked, beaten up horribly by a gang of thugs, raped, and left in the hospital half dead, defiled, violated, and with bones broken. Then I come and visit you in the hospital a few days later and say, "Be of good cheer. I have found your attackers, and I have forgiven them." What would you say to me? You would probably have a relapse right on the spot! "What right do you have to forgive them? You're not the one who was violated! You're not the one lying in a hospital bed!" Isn't that what you would say? And you would have every right to say it. Only the offended party can grant forgiveness to the perpetrator. So what right does the judge have to show these wretchedly guilty people mercy? It would be a perversion of justice.

But with God it is different. He is the judge, yet he is always the most offended party. And he never ever recuses himself. That is all right because he is never corrupted, either. His justice remains absolutely perfect. He never makes a mistake. God is not simply administering a system of morality that is bigger than he is. When we sin against God, we are not simply sinning against the law with God as a neutral observer. That is where C. H. Dodd got it so wrong. *God is the most offended party, and he is our judge!* He stands over against us in wrath righteously because he is holy, and he stands over against us in love because he is that kind of God. And he sends forth his Son to be the propitiation—the one who sets aside God's wrath—for our sins.

But this still does not quite explain how it works.

4) Paul establishes that God's justice, his righteousness, is demonstrated through the cross of Christ (3:25b–26).

God did not present Christ as a propitiation *first and foremost* to save us or to demonstrate his love. Rather: "He did this to demonstrate his *justice*, because in his forbearance he had left the sins committed beforehand unpunished" (v. 25). "The sins committed beforehand" refer not to sins that we committed prior to our conversion but to sins committed by human beings before Christ's death on the cross (hence the "but now" of 3:21). There was no *ultimate* punishment to pay for those sins. It was not until the cross that justice would be finally meted out, as verse 26 explains: God "did it to demonstrate his justice *at the present time*, so as to be just and the one who justifies those who have faith in Jesus." The cross is not only the demonstration of God's love; it is the demonstration of God's justice.

The way that Jesus propitiates his Father is in the Father's wise plan. All of God's justice is worked out in Christ, who takes our curse and penalty in his own body on the tree. That is why Christians speak of *satisfying* the wrath of God. This expression does not mean that God is up in heaven smirking, "This really satisfies me." It means that the demands of his holiness are met in the sacrifice of his own Son. His justice is *satisfied* in Jesus' propitiatory sacrifice so that all may see that sin deserves the punishment that he himself has imposed, and the punishment has been meted out. This vindicates God so that he himself is seen to be just, as well as the one who justifies the ungodly (cf. Rom. 4:5). Justification is first and foremost about the vindication of God. God simultaneously preserves his justice while justifying the ungodly. That is the heart of the gospel.

With all due respect to those who insist that penal substitution is just one gospel metaphor of many, propitiation is in fact what holds together all the other biblical ways of talking about the cross. There are two reasons for this:

1) All the other ways that the Bible speaks of the cross are tied to this one. For example, the cross reconciles us to God. Why, then, do we have to be reconciled to God? Because we are alienated from him as a

result of our sin. But does not such alienation spring from God's justice, which frowns upon our sin? What then alienates us from God? Our sin. Dealing with our sin reconciles us to God. And propitiation makes God propitious toward us, despite our sin. Again, the new birth is critical; we need a new nature by the transforming work of the Spirit. There is more to salvation than simply being forgiven. On the other hand, does God give us a new nature without reference to all the sin, ugliness, and rebellion that we have committed in the past? Or is all the power of the new nature bound up with our being reconciled to God by Christ's sacrifice? That is why the gift of the Spirit in John's Gospel is seen as flowing out from the cross. It is the gift that flows out from Christ's triumph on the cross. It is conditioned by the cross.

But it is more than that.

2) This way of looking at the cross lies at the heart of the gospel because it is embedded in the Bible's storyline. When people first sinned against God, God responded by pronouncing death (cf. the repetition of "so-and-so lived so many years, then he died" in Genesis 5). All along the Bible's storyline, God responds to sin with judgment because he is so deeply offended (e.g., the flood). The sin that above all arouses God's wrath is idolatry, the de-godding of God. "The Lord your God is a jealous God" because he alone is God. Idolatry is vertical; social sins are horizontal. All social evils exist first and foremost because humans de-god God. Sometimes in our efforts to communicate what Christianity is about we focus on the social structure of sin to show that Christianity is socially relevant, but that misses the heart of what sin really is. Although all the social manifestations of sin are horribly ugly and must be dealt with in their time and place, they must be put within the larger framework of idolatry. That is why when Paul preaches to a pagan crowd in Acts 17, he defines the problem in terms of idolatry—anything that

dethrones God, that makes humans the center and removes God from the center. In short: the drama that is unpacked by the developing story-line of the Bible puts at the center of the plot the need to be reconciled to God. And that necessarily returns us to the expiation of sin and the propitiation of God.

God presenting Christ as a propitiatory sacrifice is not an instance of "cosmic child abuse" in which God beats up on his kid.[6] We read a mere two chapters later in Romans 5:6–8, "You see, at just the right time, when we were still powerless, Christ died for the ungodly. Very rarely will anyone die for a righteous man, though for a good man someone might possibly dare to die. But God demonstrates his own love for us in this: While we were still sinners, Christ died for us." *God* demonstrates his love in that *Christ* died for us. You must not think that God stands over against us while Christ stands for us, as if Father and Son are somehow at odds, so that the Father takes it out on his Son. *God* demonstrates his love by sending Christ. This is bound up with the very nature and mystery of the incarnation and the Trinity. This is the triune God's plan. It hurts the Father to lose his Son, but he does it because he loves us. And the Son demonstrates his love for us by listening to and conforming to his Father's own wonderful plan so that this plan of the triune God is worked out in God's justice being secured and protected by virtue of the fact that *Christ* bears our sins and God's just standards are preserved even while we stand free and go forgiven. *God* demonstrates his justice in the cross.

---

[6]Contrast Steve Chalke and Alan Mann, who, dismissing the notion of penal substitution and a propitiating sacrifice, write, "The fact is that the cross isn't a form of cosmic child abuse—a vengeful father, punishing his son for an offence he has not even committed. Understandably, both people inside and outside of the church have found this twisted version of events morally dubious and a huge barrier to faith. Deeper than that, however, is that such a construct stands in total contradiction to the statement 'God is love.' If the cross is a personal act of violence perpetrated by God towards humankind but borne by his son, then it makes a mockery of Jesus' own teaching to love your enemies and refuse to repay evil with evil. The truth is the cross is a symbol of love. It is a demonstration of just how far God as Father and Jesus as his son are prepared to go to prove that love. The cross is a vivid statement of the powerlessness of love" (*The Lost Message of Jesus* [Grand Rapids: Zondervan, 2003], 182–83).

Do you want to see the greatest evidence of the love of God? Go to the cross. Do you want to see the greatest evidence of the justice of God? Go to the cross. It is where wrath and mercy meet. Holiness and peace kiss each other. The climax of redemptive history is the cross.

Because it is this God who is offended by our sin and stands over against us in judgment, and it is this God who loves us anyway, this sort of passage deals most powerfully and potently with the problem and provides the remedy. God in the fullness of time sent forth his own Son. In this one climactic sacrifice, God takes action both to punish sin and to forgive sinners. In any final sense, the sins had remained unpunished; now they are punished in the very person of the Son. And God is now both just and the one who justifies the ungodly. This is received by faith.

Do *you* believe? Or do you find yourself among the millions who begin to glimpse what the cross is about and dismiss the entire account as scandalous? A living-and-dying-and-living God? A God who stands over against us in wrath and who loves us anyway? A cross where punishment is meted out by God and borne by God? Scandalous!

And what will you do when you give an account to him on the last day, and tell him that you read this chapter or heard this message and walked away?

Conclusion

Everything that we know and appreciate and praise God for in all of Christian experience both in this life and in the life to come springs from this bloody cross.

Do we have the gift of the Spirit? Secured by Christ on the cross.

Do we enjoy the fellowship of saints? Secured by Christ on the cross.

Does he give us comfort in life and in death? Secured by Christ on the cross.

Does he watch over us faithfully, providentially, graciously, and covenantally? Secured by Christ on the cross.

Do we have hope of a heaven to come? Secured by Christ on the cross.

Do we anticipate resurrection bodies on the last day? Secured by Christ on the cross.

Is there a new heaven and a new earth, the home of righteousness? Secured by Christ on the cross.

Do we now enjoy new identities, so that we are no longer to see ourselves as nothing but failures, moral pariahs, disappointments to our parents—but as deeply loved, blood-bought, human beings, redeemed by Christ, declared just by God himself, owing to the fact that God himself presented his Son Jesus as the propitiation for our sins? All this is secured by Christ on the cross and granted to those who have faith in him.

These themes have often been picked up very powerfully by both old hymns and new ones. William Rees (1802–1883) wrote, "Here Is Love Vast as the Ocean":

On the mount of crucifixion fountains opened deep and wide.
Through the floodgates of Your mercy flowed a vast and gracious tide.
Here is love like mighty rivers poured unceasing from above.
Heaven's peace and perfect justice kissed a guilty world in love.

The themes of God's wrath, forbearance, and love barrel through Scripture and climax in the cross. Another such hymn is a 1995 contribution by Stuart Townend, "How Deep the Father's Love for Us":

Behold the Man upon a cross,
My sin upon His shoulders.

Ashamed I hear my mocking voice,
Call out among the scoffers.

It was my sin that held Him there
Until it was accomplished.
His dying breath has brought me life
I know that it is finished.

In all of our theologizing, in all of our debates about how the New
Testament uses the Old Testament and the precise meaning of inerrancy
and all the other subjects that must be addressed, do not ever lose the
heart of the issue: "God was reconciling the world to himself in Christ"
(2 Cor. 5:19).

Dilemma wretched: how shall holiness
Of brilliant life unshaded, tolerate
Rebellion's fetid slime, and not abate
In its own glory, compromised at best?
Dilemma wretched: how can truth attest
That God is love, and not be shamed by hate
And wills enslaved and bitter death—the freight
Of curse deserved, the human rebels' mess?
    The Cross! The Cross! The sacred meeting-place
    Where, knowing neither compromise nor loss,
    God's love and holiness in shattering grace
    The great dilemma slays! The Cross! The Cross!
This holy, loving God whose dear Son dies
By this is just—and one who justifies.[7]

---

[7]D. A. Carson, *Holy Sonnets of the Twentieth Century* (Grand Rapids: Baker, 1994), 101.

Now have come the salvation and the power
and the kingdom of our God,
and the authority of his Christ.
For the accuser of our brothers,
who accuses them before our God day and night,
has been hurled down.

They overcame him
by the blood of the Lamb
and by the word of their testimony;
they did not love their lives so much
as to shrink from death.

Therefore rejoice, you heavens
and you who dwell in them!
But woe to the earth and the sea,
because the devil has gone down to you!
He is filled with fury,
because he knows that his time is short.

—REVELATION 12:10–12

3

The Strange Triumph of a Slaughtered Lamb

Revelation 12

One day when my son was about three, I asked him, "Nicholas, where did you get those big, wonderful, deep-blue eyes?" He replied with all of the certainty of a three-year-old, "From God." Of course, he was right. Now he is a Marine—6 feet, 2 inches, a huge hunk. If I were to ask him today where he got those big, wonderful deep-blue eyes, he might reply with the same terms, I suppose, but he might say, "I have them because both you and Mum, though neither of you has blue eyes, must have carried the necessary recessive gene, and they combined to form my DNA."

Which answer is truer?

They are both equally true.

Which answer is more fundamental or foundational?

A second question: What caused the disastrous defeat of Jerusalem and Judah in 587 B.C.?

One might mention many factors: the rise of the Babylonian superpower; the acquisitiveness of King Nebuchadnezzar; the decline and decay of the Davidic dynasty; the tragic pride, proud arrogance, and blind stupidity of King Hezekiah several monarchs earlier in the dynasty, when he exposed the wealth of the kingdom to the Babylonian emissaries; the criminal stupidity of Zedekiah despite Jeremiah's warnings; the sins of the people that attracted God's judgment.

Or one could simply say that God did it.

Which answer is truer? They are both equally true.

Which is more fundamental or foundational?

A third question: What made Job suffer? Again, we could adduce many answers: the Sabeans, the Chaldeans, and their bands of marauding riffs; the natural elements such as the windstorm that blew down the house and killed all ten of Job's children; bereavement; the illnesses that he suffered, scraping himself on an ash pit; a nagging wife; the false comfort of insensitive and theologically perverse friends.

Or one could say that Satan did it. One could even say that God did it, for Satan did not go one step beyond what God himself sanctioned.

Which answer is the most true?

They are all equally true.

Which is most fundamental or foundational?

A final question: What has caused the church her greatest sufferings during the last several decades? Of course, answers will vary enormously with location. In China, for instance, Marxist totalitarianism with a Chinese face surfaces from time to time in regional repression of Christians. This has certainly been a significant factor in the feelings of pressure that the church faces there, at least outside the special economic zones. By contrast, in many parts of sub-Saharan Africa, the church has been part of tribalism and the endless petty wars that tribalism generates, sometimes breaking out in horrendous bloodbaths. This is the residue of the colonial period that drew boundaries for the convenience of the former colonial powers without regard to tribal affinities. The inability of these countries to move toward a stable form of government that does not get overthrown a few years later by the next tribal movement or military takeover signals the absence of strong legal and constitutional traditions, not to mention the shortage of trained leadership.

The rapid urbanization of many populations and the growth of tertiary education in many African countries have also fueled the church's challenges. In urban settings in central Africa, a common saying is, "The pew is higher than the pulpit." In other words, in the urban areas there is a new generation of young, well-trained Africans who have had university education, while too many of the pastors have received only a fifth-, sixth-, seventh-, or eighth-grade education with a little Bible on top of that. I have not yet mentioned pressures from AIDS: not fewer than twelve million Africans have the HIV virus. In some villages of Uganda and Tanzania, entire populations between the ages of fifteen and sixty-five have been decimated. They call it the skinny disease. Not long ago I was in Soweto, in South Africa, where pastors regularly hold seven or eight funerals a week for AIDS victims. One could mention drought in the Sahel. Especially important is the rising tension with militant Islam in the bordering states like Sudan, Nigeria, and Eritrea. In short, Christians in Africa, though great in numbers, are weak in leadership, training, and vision for the future.

And what shall we say of the West? Here the church faces another set of challenges. Here we find material prosperity, despite the recession, coupled with (in some parts of the country) an astonishing, even an appalling, poverty. The rapid pace of life often squeezes what is important to the periphery: the urgent displaces the important, the digital displaces the personal. The mass media affect our thinking whether we like it or not, leaving us entertained, titillated, or, ironically, bored, while Madison Avenue establishes our self-identity in many things, as long as none of them has eternal significance. The pressures of secularization allow us to be religious provided our religion does not really matter: even Christian faith is funneled into privacy. It is hard to believe that a bare one hundred twenty years ago (the late 1800s) the media cabled

Charles Spurgeon's Sunday sermons to New York to be published in the Monday morning edition of the *New York Times*. People wanted the whole Spurgeon sermon printed in the press on Monday morning for their breakfast.

Can you imagine that today? Even at the level of reading, there were at the time literally hundreds of small publishing houses that produced poetry books. Hard to believe, isn't it? People then would sit down and read a volume of poetry the way they might sit down now and watch a program on TV. Today the national discourse concerns economics, politics, sports, international affairs that are of interest to us, and media stars who have become powerful for no other reason than that they are in the media. *But the national discourse rarely concerns truth, integrity, or God; or, if it does talk about God, it does not really talk about God but about the response of various people to people who talk about God.*

One hundred fifty years ago one could not discuss any item at the national level without bringing up questions of providence and what God is doing in history. Today even to raise the topic of providence makes one sound old-fashioned and vaguely irrelevant. Many in our society have been taught that in the religious realm the only view that is wrong is the view that says that any other view is wrong. The only heresy is to insist that there is such a thing as heresy. Compound such social trends with moral and theological indifferentism and prayerlessness in many of our churches, and it is easy to detect widespread malaise. And the church is suffering on account of it.

But have you noticed the categories we have used in this discussion of what ails the church in the West? They are all sociological, historical, occasional, demographic, economic, psychological, medical. They are all performance-related, circumstance-related. There is nothing about the Devil—and nothing about God.

I am certainly not suggesting that there is nothing to be learned from sociological and demographic analysis. Such analysis is helpful not only for missionaries who go to another culture to learn the language, customs, and mores of the people (their habits, biases, sense of humor, etc.) but also to help us understand our own culture, not least when our culture is changing quickly. In addition to categories like baby boomers and baby busters, Generation X, and Generation Y, most of our cities now boast many different ethnicities, movements, economic strata, and so on. It is helpful to know what is going on in the minds of university students before you evangelize them. It really is a valuable exercise to ask and answer these sorts of questions.

But if all of our *analyses* are restricted exclusively to such categories, the huge danger is that our *solutions* will be cast in such categories too. Our answers will be superficially sociological because we do not probe deeply enough to analyze the cosmic tension between God and the Devil. And then, quite frankly, we do not really need God. He could get up and walk out, and we would not miss him. We have got this thing taped; our analyses are quantifiable.

In the chapter before us (Revelation 12), John provides us with a glimpse of the church's problems from God's perspective. The literary genre he uses is apocalyptic. That genre sometimes seems strange to us today because it is no longer written (though it was common enough in Jewish and Christian circles from about 300 B.C. to about A.D. 300, with tentacles reaching back much earlier). Apocalyptic literature uses colorful arrays of symbols and metaphors to analyze human situations from the perspective of heaven. If I understand the passage before us aright, God here gives us a deeper analysis of the difficulties and sufferings of the church, and then teaches us something of how to be faithful.

Revelation 12 to 14 marks a major division in the Apocalypse. These chapters constitute a major hiatus before the final display of God's wrath in the seven plagues of Revelation 16. John traces in these chapters the underlying cause for the hostility and suffering that fall upon the church. That cause is nothing less than the rage of Satan against the church. If you do not have a category for Satan's rage, John says, then you cannot understand deeply what is happening in contemporary Christianity.

John Outlines the Occasion for This Satanic Rage (Rev. 12:1–9)

In John's vision the scene opens with a great and wondrous sign appearing in heaven. "Sign" here, as elsewhere in the book of Revelation and occasionally in the OT, refers to a great spectacle that points in some way to the consummation. The content of this sign or spectacle is a woman, and what a woman she is: "a woman clothed with the sun, with the moon under her feet and a crown of twelve stars on her head" (v. 1).

Who is she? Some across church history have suggested that she is Mary because she gives birth to "a son, a male child, who 'will rule all the nations with an iron scepter'" (v. 5). The son in verse 5 clearly refers to Jesus. But the view that the woman is Mary is refuted a little farther on, in verse 17 (not infrequently in apocalyptic literature a symbol is introduced and then unpacked later): "Then the dragon was enraged at the woman and went off to make war against the rest of her offspring—those who keep God's commands and hold fast their testimony about Jesus." Here the woman cannot be Mary. This woman is the messianic community as a whole, whether under the old covenant or the new. Just as Israel under the old covenant is symbolically understood to be the mother of the people of God (e.g., Isa. 54:1—"Sing, barren woman"—is addressed to Zion=Jerusalem), so under the new covenant, the heavenly Jerusalem is our mother: "the Jerusalem that is above is free, and she is our mother"

(Gal. 4:26). The Messiah springs from this mother, out of this woman, out of this messianic community. The messianic community gives birth to this child, and then the messianic community continues. The messianic community's children are the ones being persecuted in Revelation 12:17—and this side of the cross, the messianic community's children are Christians.

The woman is "clothed with the sun" (v. 1); she is utterly radiant. Her feet on the moon suggest dominion. The "twelve stars on her head" are probably evocative of both the twelve tribes of the old covenant and the twelve apostles of the new, representing the fullness of the people of God. (Jesus links these two groups of twelve in Matthew 19.)

But the important thing for the drama is that she is pregnant: "She was pregnant and cried out in pain as she was about to give birth" (v. 2). Descriptions such as this generated the expression "the birth pains of the Messiah." This expression did not refer to the pains that the Messiah himself suffered, but the pains of the messianic community as the Messiah came to birth. Such sentiments are grounded in Old Testament pictures and realities. For example, Isaiah 26:17:

> As a pregnant woman about to give birth
> writhes and cries out in her pain,
> so were we in your presence, LORD.

Thus, it was understood before the Messiah came that the people of God (the woman in Revelation 12) would go through the birth pains of the Messiah. She is in travail, pregnant, waiting for the coming of the Messiah.

The old covenant community gives birth to the Messiah, and this community continues after the Messiah is born; the old community remains in connection with the new community (Rev. 12:17). So what we have in these opening verses is true Israel, the messianic community, in an agony of suffering and expectation as the Messiah comes to birth. That is the first sign or spectacle.

The second spectacle is an enormous red dragon (v. 3). If we have any doubts about who or what the red dragon is, verse 9 identifies him as "that ancient serpent called the devil, or Satan, who leads the whole world astray." Dragon, leviathan, monster of the deep—these are standard symbols for all that opposes God, and sometimes for the Devil himself. Sometimes these creatures manifest themselves in historic entities. Thus the dragon or Satan is associated with Egypt in connection with the exodus (Psalm 74), elsewhere with Assyria and Babylon (Isaiah 27), Pharaoh (Ezekiel 29), and even Peter (Matthew 16 and parallels). You will recall the context of this last-named incident. Jesus asks, "Who do people say the Son of Man is?" (Matt. 16:13). Peter, prompted by God himself, replies, "You are the Christ, the Son of the living God" (v. 16). Jesus responds, "Blessed are you, Simon son of Jonah, for this was not revealed to you by man, but by my Father in heaven" (v. 17). And from that point on he then speaks more clearly of his impending death and resurrection.

But that is too much for Peter. By his lights, a crucified Messiah is a contradiction in terms. Having scored once and received praise from the Master, he tries to score again: "Never, Lord! This shall never happen to you!" (v. 22). Peter recoiled at the notion that the Messiah would have to die, but Jesus wheels on him: "Get behind me, *Satan!*" (v. 23). Jesus is certainly not saying that Peter's mind has clicked off and that he has been taken over by Satan himself (i.e., that he is demon-possessed). Rather, Peter is speaking what *Peter* thinks; Peter is giving his considered judgment. This is Peter's utterance and folly. But Peter's judgment is diabolical and wrongheaded in that it fails to understand that the Messiah is also the suffering Servant. Thus, the voice behind Peter's voice is Satan's. It reflects Satan's blinding, deceiving, destroying work. Peter's judgment is fundamentally false when it should have been right. It was Satan's work as it was Satan's work behind Pharaoh, Egypt, Assyria, Babylon, and myriads of forms today.

Satan is a "*red* dragon" (Rev. 12:3), almost certainly a symbol for blood, for his murderousness, recalling the words of Jesus: "He was a murderer from the beginning" (John 8:44). By Satan's work the entire human race died.

The dragon has "seven heads" (Rev. 12:3). Apocalyptic often has mixed metaphors: seven heads, ten horns, seven crowns. Apparently the ten horns are not evenly distributed on the seven heads! This is not something to be taken literally. Like Leviathan's multiple heads in Psalm 74:14, the "seven heads" refer to the universality of his power; he "leads the whole world astray" (Rev. 12:9).

Horns typically signify kings or king-dominion: awesome power and kingly authority. This recalls the fourth beast of Daniel 7.

The crowns on his head are not victory wreaths but crowns of arrogated, usurped authority against him who is in fact rightly the one who "will rule all the nations with an iron scepter" (Rev. 12:5), the King of kings and the Lord of lords.

The dragon's tail, we are told, "swept a third of the stars out of the sky and flung them to the earth" (v. 4). This is not some form of mistaken ancient cosmology demonstrating that the biblical authors were woefully ignorant of scientific facts. Rather, this is part of apocalyptic metaphor that derives from Hebrew poetry in which all of nature gets involved in everything. When things go well, the hills dance and the trees clap their hands. When things are bad, the stars fall from the sky, and nature falls into disarray. This is exactly what happens here. Satan is about to attempt something that is utterly catastrophic, so his tail swings around and a third of the universe collapses. The language is drawn from Daniel 8:9–10.

What is Satan trying to do? The scene is grotesque. The dragon stands in front of the woman. She is lying there in labor. Her feet are in the stirrups, writhing as she pushes to give birth, and this disgusting dragon is waiting to grab the baby as it comes out of the birth canal and then eat it (12:4). The scene is meant to be grotesque: it reflects the implacable rage of Satan against the arriving Messiah.

Do we not know how this works out in historical terms? The first bloodbath in the time of Jesus takes place in the little village of Bethlehem—in the slaughter of the innocents as Herod tries to squash this baby's perceived threat to his throne. Jesus is saved by Joseph, who is warned by God in a dream and flees to Egypt. Herod, in a rage, "gave orders to kill all the boys in Bethlehem and its vicinity who were two years old and under" (Matt. 2:16). Satan later manifests his rage against Jesus in the temptation, and he manifests his rage against the church in every temptation. Satan's rage manifests itself when some people try to push Jesus over a cliff, and others take up stones to stone him. Satan is after Jesus and wants to destroy him by any means possible. Behind all these attempts to destroy Jesus is the red dragon, and behind the red dragon is God himself, bringing to pass his purposes even in the death of his Son to bring about our redemption.

But the text does not go on to talk about Jesus' triumph here, not because this book has no interest in him but because the triumph of Jesus has already been spectacularly introduced in Revelation 4–5. The great vision of Revelation 4–5 controls the entire book. There we learn that Christ, this male child, is the only one who is fit to open the scroll in God's right hand to bring about all of God's purposes for judgment and blessing. He is the Lion and the Lamb, the reigning king and the bloody sacrifice, the heir to David's throne yet the one who appears from God's throne. Because of his struggle, men and women from every tongue and tribe and people and nation are redeemed. Countless millions gather around him who sits on the throne and the Lamb and sing a new song of adoring, grateful, praise.

But here in Revelation 12 we move from Jesus' birth to his ascension; we run through his entire life, ministry, death, resurrection, and ascension in two lines: he "will rule all the nations with an iron scepter" and "was snatched up to God and to his throne" (v. 5). The male child, Jesus, is born and snatched to heaven. In other words, this passage focuses not on Christ's triumph—that is presupposed—but on what happens to the woman and her children, the ones left behind. And that is us: the messianic community, the people of God, the blood-bought church of Jesus Christ. This side of the cross they are described as "those who obey God's commands and hold the testimony of Jesus" (v. 17). The woman (the messianic community) is the focus of the passage.

The woman flees to the wilderness for 1,260 days (v. 6). There are two elements of great importance here: the significance of the wilderness and of the 1,260 days.

1) *The significance of the wilderness.* The messianic community—the church—flees to the wilderness. What would that mean to a first-century Christian reader?

The wilderness is the place through which the messianic community of the old covenant passed on the way to the Promised Land. As such, it was a time of testing, difficulty, temptation, and judgment. It was not yet the Promised Land. It was the desert. But at the same time, it was the place where God had so miraculously provided for his people that later prophets could look back on it as a time of intimacy, wooing, and winning. There God performed wonderful miracles: water from a rock, the provision of manna and quail, the preservation of their shoes. God taught them wonderful lessons in revealed words and spectacular miracles. Because of God's faithfulness to his covenant community as they passed through the desert on the way to the Promised Land, the same expression is picked up later by the prophets. Thus in Hosea 2, when the people of God are again betraying him and committing spiritual adultery, God says, "Therefore I am now going to allure her; I will lead her *into the desert* and speak tenderly to her" (Hos. 2:14). The wilderness was not only the place of trial and testing; it is also the place where God led his people with the tender wooing affections of a courtier. God is winning his people, cherishing them, drawing them to himself, saving them, protecting them until the consummation, and preparing them for the move into the Promised Land.

That is what is going on here in verse 6 and a little later in the chapter. The woman flees to the desert to get away from Satan. The desert is scarcely hospitable, but it is prepared for the woman by God. God is nurturing his own people in the desert afresh in preparation for the consummation (the ultimate Promised Land). So also in the church's experience today: we may have to go through terrible hardships, but those hardships are accompanied by the wonderful, wooing, grace of God.

2) *The significance of the 1,260 days.* What does "1,260 days" mean? There have been endless speculations and dogmatic assertions about various interpretations.

A good place to start is recognition that many cultures have in their history a specified period of time that carries a symbol-laden value. I am a Canadian by birth, but I have lived in America for three decades. My children were born here and have attended American schools. Even I, a foreigner, know that the overwhelming majority of Americans would instantly know where this number comes from: "fourscore and seven years." Regardless of whether you are from the North or the South, you know when and where those words were spoken. They come from the first sentence of what is perhaps the most remarkable speech in American history: "Fourscore and seven years ago our fathers brought forth, upon this continent, a new nation, conceived in Liberty, and dedicated to the proposition that all men are created equal." In other words, Abraham Lincoln's Gettysburg Address has become stamped on the psychology of the American schoolchild, whether white, black, Asian, or Latin-American—it does not matter. It is part of the American heritage, and it is inseparably linked to the Civil War and its entailments. It is part of American mythology.

In Israel, the period of time with corresponding mythic power was three and a half years. Two centuries before Christ, there arose one of the most grisly episodes in Jewish history, an episode foreseen by Daniel. In the book of Revelation, the crucial period of time is indicated by four synonymous expressions: forty-two months (based on the ideal month of thirty days), 1,260 days, three and a half years, and time (i.e., one year), times (i.e., two years), and half a time (i.e., one-half of a year); see 11:2–3; 12:6, 14; 13:5. They refer to the same thing and share the same significance. For Jewish and Christian readers in the first century, this period of immense suffering instantly calls to mind the wretched reign of Antiochus IV Epiphanes.

A little history explains why he was such an important figure. After the people of God began to return to the Promised Land (i.e., after the exile), eventually the old Persian Empire broke up, crushed by the Greeks. Then the Greek empire fell apart as well. It was divided into four parts, each ruled by one of the four senior generals of Alexander the Great. One of those generals started the Ptolemaic dynasty in Egypt;

another started the Seleucid dynasty in Syria. Little Israel was squashed between those two opposing powers, and it was forced to curry favor with each side, scrambling incessantly to support whichever side seemed to be in the ascendancy. In this period, however, Israel was never independent. It was a no-man's land for decade after decade of ruthless, bloodthirsty, recurrent, strife.

By 167 B.C., the Seleucids in Syria, to the north, finally won control over Israel. The Seleucid king was Antiochus IV Epiphanes, a cruel and bloody man. He determined to crush all forms of Jewish worship, to force-feed paganism to Israel and establish Hellenistic religions. He moved his armies into Jerusalem. He sacrificed pigs in the new temple in Jerusalem. He made it a capital offense to observe any Jewish rite such as circumcision or the Sabbath, to own or read any part of Scripture, or to be a priest.

So the slaughter began. The emissaries of Antiochus IV Epiphanes murdered many people, including many priests. In due course the troops arrived at a small village in the hill country of Judea and encountered an old priest named Mattathias. When one of the emissaries approached him, Mattathias killed him. Mattathias had three sons. One was Judas Maccabeus (Judas "the hammer"). Judas Maccabeus began a campaign of guerrilla warfare. Doubtless others had adopted this tactic at an earlier period, but his guerrilla tactics are the first detailed descriptions of guerrilla warfare we have (e.g., hiding in the hills and hit-and-run attacks). Josephus records the struggle in some detail. After *three and a half years* of bloody warfare (the Maccabean Revolt), there was finally a pitched battle on the shores of the Orontes River, and the Jews soundly defeated the Syrians and rededicated the temple in 164 B.C. For the first time in more than four hundred years, Israel was an independent nation.

Because that three-and-a-half-year period was such a burning memory in the Jews' mind from that point on (and they understood it in connection with their interpretation of Daniel), they came to think of three and a half years as a time of severe testing, opposition, and tribulation before God himself gave his people rest again. That is what is being said here in Revelation 12. This woman flees into the desert and faces a time of testing, opposition, and tribulation for a constrained period of time before God himself comes and gives final release. "If those days had not been cut short, no one would survive" (Matt. 24:22a).

Thus, for Jews and Christians alike, three and a half years became emblematic of a period of intense suffering (of whatever duration) before God manifests himself in saving power. Of course, when John was writing this book, the Maccabean Revolt was more than two centuries behind him, but the point is that the 1,260 days had become emblematic for any period of severe suffering. John uses the expression to refer to the *entire* period of suffering between Jesus' first and second advents. It is the period when there will be suffering, opposition, attack, and death. But ultimately there will be vindication at the end as God moves in.

Meanwhile the events in heaven mirror the events on earth (Rev. 12:7–9). The dragon fights angelic beings and is cast out. This is equivalent to Jesus' own teaching: "I saw Satan fall like lightning from heaven" (Luke 10:18). With the onset of the Messianic ministry, Satan is banished from heaven. When Jesus says this during his ministry, he does so in connection with the preaching and displays of power of the gospel itself as it is promulgated through his own appointed disciples—all of this in anticipation of the cross and resurrection that are just around the corner. "I saw Satan fall like lightning from heaven." So also hear: "The great dragon was hurled down—that ancient serpent called the devil, or Satan, who leads the whole world astray" (Rev. 12:9). The decisive turning point has taken place; he is defeated in principle. That happened at the cross, resurrection, and exaltation of Jesus, at the dawning of the kingdom of God.

This is a major theme in Scripture. In Job, for instance, Satan appears in the presence of God along with "the sons of God"—other angelic beings. It is almost as if Satan has access to God at that point precisely because the redeeming work of Christ is not yet done. Satan is "the accuser of our brothers" (12:10): "You see, God, this Job character claims to be devoted to you only because you have nurtured him. He is actually a rotter. In his heart he will curse you to your face if you merely take away some of the protection with which you have shielded him." And thus the drama of the book of Job begins.

But now Satan is cast out of heaven. The accuser of the brothers and sisters is gone. Why? There has been war in heaven, and he has been cast out. The reason he has been cast out is the triumph of Christ. Satan has no basis for such accusation anymore. Why? Because a redeemer has arisen.

That becomes the basis for the next turn in the argument. As we shall see, the central point of the next verses, cast in poetic form, is that the accuser of our brothers and sisters has been hurled down (vv. 10, 12).

John Identifies the Reasons for This Satanic Rage (Rev. 12:10, 12–17)

Satan's sphere is now restricted, and his time is short (12:10, 12–13).

Once Satan has been hurled to the earth (v. 9), John "heard a loud voice in heaven say: 'Now have come the salvation and the power and the kingdom of our God, and the authority of his Christ'" (v. 10a). The kingdom has dawned. It is here. It is not yet consummated, but it is now come. It has started. One of the ways in which this has been demonstrated is that Satan himself has been decisively defeated. Or in terms of the symbolism of 12:7–9, Satan has been cast out of heaven. He has no standing before God whatsoever. He cannot bring accusations against the brothers anymore, "for the accuser of our brothers, who accuses them before our God day and night, has been hurled down" (v. 10b). Satan, though doubtless he has been operating on the earth since the beginning of the creation, is now restricted to the earth and has lost his access to God that had enabled him to accuse us before God so directly.

So Satan turns all his rage and vengeance upon the woman (i.e., upon *us*, the messianic community): "When the dragon saw that he had been hurled to the earth, he pursued the woman who had given birth to the male child" (v. 13). It is precisely the Devil's restriction in authority that is the fundamental reason here for his rage in this restricted sphere. Satan is not only wicked; he is frustrated, angry, and vituperative. "He is filled with fury, because he knows that his time is short" (v. 12). Satan is full of rage not because he is so spectacularly strong, but because he knows that he is defeated, his end is in sight, the range of his operations is curtailed—and he is furious. He knows that in principle he is already undone.

This reaction is psychologically believable because it has happened many times in history. For instance, during the Gulf War, once the allies had arrived with a quarter of a million troops, tons of materiel, and sophisticated weapons that Saddam Hussein could not possibly match, anyone with half a brain in his head knew that it was over. It was uncertain how bloody it might be and what setbacks might be encountered, but it was over. Does that mean that Saddam Hussein quit? No, he ordered his troops to fight, and they were killed and captured by the thousands. They fired all the oil wells in Kuwait on their way out. Saddam did the most vengeful things when it was clear that he was already beaten. It was not rational, yet his response was not atypical for defeated despots.

Is this not what Hitler did in World War II? By 1944, the Germans were losing ground on the eastern front. At tremendous cost, the Russians were pressing against them. The other allies had cleaned out North Africa and landed on the boot of Italy and were coming up the boot. Then in June, on D-Day, the troops landed on the beaches of Normandy. Within three days they had pumped in 1.1 million troops and tons of war materiel. Anybody with half a brain in his head and an ounce of historical knowledge could see that the war was over and that Hitler was finished. In terms of resources, numbers of soldiers, money (on which war finally turns), energy, and supplies, the war was over. It was not just a matter of who was winning this or that battle. Japan could turn out about seven tons of steel a year; Germany was being bombed flat and could not produce more than thirteen or fourteen tons. America alone was producing fifty to sixty tons. The figures were all on the allies' side. Just give it time. Hitler was finished. Does that mean that Hitler quit? That is what most of his generals wanted him to do. But no, after that came the Battle of the Bulge and then the assault on Berlin—some of the worst fighting of the war. Hitler knew that his time was short, but he did not quit; it merely filled him with increased rage.

That is the nature of the opposition we face. Satan's sphere is restricted, his time is short, and he is angry. He cannot get directly at Jesus, so he aims to do as much damage as he possibly can to Jesus' people, to the woman; that is, to you and me. The troubles of Christ's people (the children of the woman) arise not because Satan is too strong but because he is beaten in principle and will rage violently to the very end. Our present conflict belongs to this cosmic scope.

Moreover, Satan's success will be limited (12:13–17).

Much of the description of Satan's attack on the people of God, along with the defensive moves that God takes to protect his people, are cast in terms of events that took place in the years of Israel's wilderness wandering. "The woman was given the two wings of a great eagle, so that she might fly to the place prepared for her in the desert" (v. 14a). This is probably picking up language from Exodus 19:4: "You yourselves have seen what I did to Egypt, and how I carried you on eagles' wings and brought you to myself." Revelation 13:14–17 evokes many similar bits of exodus typology. The woman is borne along by God himself to the wilderness introduced in 12:6.

"She would be taken care of for a time, times and half a time, out of the serpent's reach" (v. 14b). There it is again: a period of testing before the final release. Does this mean that the woman really is "out of the serpent's reach"? Is there no more trouble to worry about? No, the serpent is busy chasing her, so he tries to drown her by spewing "water like a river, to overtake the woman and sweep her away with the torrent" (v. 15). This is almost certainly a reference to Exodus 1–2, where again Satan, using Pharaoh, tried to sweep away the entire promised line, commanding that every male child be drowned in the Nile River. Again, Satan wants the church destroyed.

But God is not finished. "The earth helped the woman by opening its mouth and swallowing the river that the dragon had spewed out of his mouth" (Rev. 12:16). Does that mean that the Devil quits? No, he is even more enraged: "Then the dragon was enraged at the woman and went off to make war against the rest of her offspring—those who obey God's commands and hold the testimony of Jesus" (v. 17). If we went on to read the next chapter (Revelation 13), we would discover that Satan has two important cohorts: the antichrist and the false prophet, one connected with the sea and the other with the land. Satan's domain is limited to the land and the sea (12:12), and so in Revelation 13 the beasts come out of the land and the sea and constitute, with Satan himself, an unholy triumvirate, the Satanic trinity: Satan, the beast out of the land, and the beast out of the sea. How Satan works out this opposition through his cohorts is unpacked in the next two chapters.

The reasons for Satan's rage are clear: his sphere is restricted, his time is short, and his success is limited. The current conflict the church faces must be understood, for it is ours. This is where we live and move and have our being.

Before we press on, it is worth pausing to ask how this titanic struggle between Satan and the church is faring. Even if we know that Christ and his people will ultimately win, what is the state of play right now? Throughout the history of the Christian church, various theories have been advanced as to whether the world is getting better or worse. They are tied up with large schemes of eschatology (the doctrine of last things). In the Puritan period, the majority of Puritan pastors were post-millennialists; they believed that eventually a time of millennial splendor and glory before the Lord's final return would be introduced by the preaching of the gospel. The postmillennialists believed that they were entering into a golden age of such magnificent earth-transforming power as the gospel was heralded afresh with renewed vigor, that in effect Christ would rule through his Word, through the church, and thus introduce an age of great missionary outreach and glory that could only be called millennial. It did not work out that way.

I remember reading, in 1993, the important book by Francis Fukuyama, *The End of History and the Last Man*. Fukuyama's thesis at the time (he has since revised it) was that with the fall of the Berlin Wall in 1989, the major world conflicts were over. That was the sense of his dictum, that history was coming to an end. He did not mean *literally* that time had stopped but that the major world conflicts were now over. Liberal democracy was gradually going to win. Oh, yes, for hundreds of years there might be local skirmishes of one sort or another, but there was little possibility of another intercontinental war, another world war. The big wars had come to an end, liberal democracy had won, and we had reached the end of history. That is a kind of secular version of postmillennialism: world peace, not through the gospel, but through liberal democracy. I remember reading that book and thinking, "My dear Fukuyama, either you are right or Jesus is right, but you are not both right because Jesus said that all along there will be wars and rumors of wars" (Matt. 24:6).

By contrast, at other times in the history of the church Christians have fastened their attention on moral and cultural declension. Everything appears to be decaying. We are in one of those periods today in the Western world (though not in every part of the world). The voices of gloom tell us that the culture is declining, moral standards are eroding, integrity is disappearing. So now another set of biblical texts is commonly cited. Rather than saying, "For the earth will be filled with the knowledge of the glory of the Lord as the waters cover the sea" (Hab. 2:14; cf. Isa. 11:9), we relegate that prospect to the new heaven and the new earth. We prefer to quote, "Evil men and impostors will go from bad to worse, deceiving and being deceived" (2 Tim. 3:13). The world is going to get worse. The context of the latter verse, however, shows us that what is in Paul's mind is not that each generation will be worse than the preceding generations but that evil people in every generation will become worse and worse.

So what, then, is the truth of the matter? In this massive struggle between the church of Jesus Christ and the rage of Satan himself, how is the fight going?

One of the most insightful ways of considering this question is to think through Jesus' parable of the wheat and the weeds (Matt. 13:24–30):

> Jesus told them another parable: "The kingdom of heaven is like a man who sowed good seed in his field. But while everyone was sleeping, his enemy came and sowed weeds among the wheat, and went away. When the wheat sprouted and formed heads, then the weeds also appeared.
>
> "The owner's servants came to him and said, 'Sir, didn't you sow good seed in your field? Where then did the weeds come from?'
>
> "'An enemy did this,' he replied.
>
> "The servants asked him, 'Do you want us to go and pull them up?'
>
> "'No,' he answered, 'because while you are pulling the weeds, you may uproot the wheat with them. *Let both grow together until the harvest.* At that time I will tell the harvesters: First collect the weeds and tie them in bundles to be burned; then gather the wheat and bring it into my barn.'"

Jesus acknowledges that an enemy has done this, but he insists that both wheat and weeds must grow until the end.

By virtually any calculation, in the last 150 years there has been greater international mission work and more conversions to Christ than in the preceding 1,800 years combined. The gospel has gone to more people and places than ever before. On the other hand, there have been more Christian martyrs in the last 150 years than in the preceding 1,800 years combined.

So what will happen in the twenty-first century? I am neither a prophet nor the son of a prophet, but I will tell you what will happen if Jesus does not come back first: the world will continue to get both better and worse. The gospel will advance, and so will opposition. Christians will sow the gospel seed, and there will be outbreaks of revival and blessing here and there, times of sowing and harvesting that gather millions and millions of people. There will be a great ingathering along with great persecution, perhaps the greatest persecution that we have ever faced. This will not happen all at once entirely in the same place at the same time, but the King has declared, "Let both grow together until the harvest."

There will be wars and rumors of wars, so do not be alarmed; the end is not yet (Matt. 24:6). Satan is filled with fury, and he knows his time is short. It is poppycock to expect that things will only get better and that we will experience world peace if we have the right kind of president or policy. Do people not read history anymore? That utopian idealism is exactly what Woodrow Wilson wanted after World War I; hence the League of Nations. The result was World War II.

Do not misunderstand me. Not for a moment am I suggesting that there are not better or worse policies to follow, or that Christians should not be involved in the play for peace. I am suggesting, however, that to have a Pollyannaish view of history and human nature is deeply unbiblical. Worse: beyond all of the faults and failures and betrayals of human nature is the rage of Satan, who deludes the peoples of the world. He is full of fury because he knows that his time is short.

Our eschatological visions are too often constrained by our own narrow place in history. We do not take the broader view. Above all, we do not sufficiently submit to the explicit teaching of the Lord Jesus: "Let both grow together until the harvest."

We have considered, then, some of the reasons for Satan's rage and briefly glanced at the consequence. But now, at last, some good news.

John Specifies How Christians Overcome This Satanic Rage (Rev. 12:11)

Verses 10 and 11 must be read together, for verse 10 is the crucial setting for verse 11:

Then I heard a loud voice in heaven say:

"Now have come the salvation and the power
    and the kingdom of our God,
    and the authority of his Christ.
For the accuser of our brothers,
    who accuses them before our God day and night,
    has been hurled down.
They overcame him
    by the blood of the Lamb
    and by the word of their testimony;
they did not love their lives so much
    as to shrink from death."

The setting (v. 10) reminds us that what is in view is the triumph of Christ, the onset of his reign, the dawning of Messiah's kingdom—and it is coincidental with Satan's destruction, with his being hurled out of heaven and, in subsequent verses, opening up his onslaught against Christians.

So what are the Christians to do about it? How do the offspring of the woman cope with this satanic rage? Three things are said of these believers:

They overcame him by (i.e., on the ground of) the blood of the Lamb (Rev. 12:11a).

The great redemptive act that freed them from their sins (1:5) and established their right to reign as priests and kings (5:9) is also what gives them authority over Satan and enables them to overcome Satan and all of his accusations (12:11). Satan accuses Christians day and night. It is not just that he will work on our conscience to make us feel as dirty, guilty, defeated, destroyed, weak, and ugly as he possibly can; it is something worse: his entire ploy in the past is to accuse us *before God* day and night, bringing charges against us that we know we can never answer before the majesty of God's holiness. What can we say in response? Will our defense be, "Oh, I'm not that bad!"? You will never beat Satan that way. Never. What you must say is, "Satan, I'm even worse than you think, but God loves me anyway. He has accepted me because of the blood of the Lamb."

The preposition in the original here is very important. The English expression *by* might sound as if "the blood of the Lamb" is instrumental (*by* or *through* the blood of the Lamb), but the original is quite clear that they overcame him *on the ground* of "the blood of the Lamb." The blood of the Lamb is the *ground* of our victory, not simply the *means* in some mechanical sense.

All Christian blessings and resources are grounded in the blood of the Lamb. From a Christian perspective, all the blessings and resources that are ours in Christ are grounded in the blood of the Lamb; they are secured by Jesus' death and resurrection.

Do you find yourself accepted before this holy God? If so, it is because of the blood of the Lamb. Have you received the blessed Holy Spirit? He has been poured out because of the blood of the Lamb. Do you have the prospect of consummated eternal life in glory? It was secured by the blood of the Lamb. Are you in the fellowship of saints, brothers and sisters who love Christ, the church of the living God, a new body, the body of Christ on earth? This is bought, secured, and constituted by the blood of the Lamb. Are you grateful for the spiritual armaments that Paul tells us to deploy (Ephesians 6)? The entire arsenal is at our disposal because of the blood of the Lamb. May we go to God in prayer? It is because of the blood of the Lamb. Do we find our wills strengthened by the Spirit? That incalculable benefit was secured by the blood of the Lamb.

Every whiff of victory over the principalities and powers of this dark age has been secured by the blood of the Lamb.

Picture two Jews with the remarkable names of Smith and Jones. They live in the land of Goshen almost a millennium and a half before Christ. It is early evening, and they are talking to each other near the end of the ten plagues. Mr. Smith says to Mr. Jones, "Mr. Jones, have you daubed the two doorposts and the lintel with the blood of the lamb tonight?"

Mr. Jones replies, "Oh, yes, I certainly have. You heard what Moses said. The angel of death is passing through the land. Some of the plagues have afflicted just the Egyptians, but some of them have been over the whole land. Moses insisted that this plague was going to run throughout the entire land of Goshen where we live, as well as the rest of Egypt. The firstborn of people and of cattle are going to be killed. The only exceptions are in those homes that have been daubed with lamb's blood, the way Moses prescribed." He pauses and then adds, "I'm really excited about this because this means that our redemption is drawing near. Of course, I've slaughtered the lamb. My friends and relatives are all here, and we're ready to go. I've daubed the blood of the lamb on the two doorposts and on the lintel. How about you, Mr. Smith?"

Mr. Smith replies, "Well, of course, I've done the same thing. But boy, am I worried. Have you seen the things that have gone on around here the last few months? Frogs, lice, hail, death. Now Moses is talking about every firstborn. Look, I've got only one son; you've got three. I love my Charlie, and I don't want to lose him. I'm scared witless. There's not going to be any sleep for me tonight."

Rather surprised, Mr. Jones replies, "What are you worried about? God himself has promised through his servant Moses that if you daub the blood on the two doorposts and on the lintel, you are saved. Your child will be saved. Charlie will be here tomorrow morning. You've already put the blood on the two doorposts and on the lintel."

Mr. Smith replies, "Well, you've got that last bit right. I've certainly done that, but I'm scared witless just the same."

That night the angel of death passes through the land. Who loses his son? Mr. Smith or Mr. Jones?

The answer, of course, is neither—because the promise was based not on the intensity of their faith nor on the joy of their obedience but on whether they hid under the blood of the lamb.

Let's come at this another way. Do you ever have a day that runs something like this? You get up in the morning; it is drizzly and hot, and the air conditioner is broken. You reach for a clean, fresh pair of socks, and you can't find two that match. You stub your toe on that nail sticking out of the wall that you knew you should have fixed about three years ago. You cut yourself while you are shaving. You stumble down to breakfast, and that day your wife is going out for a special meeting with her friends and has not done anything. You go out to the car, put your key in the ignition, and it will not start. You knew that you should have had the battery checked, and it is deader than a dodo. You get to work late, and people are saying rude things about you. Then your boss says, "Have you finished that report yet? You're staying late tonight if you haven't." The whole day unfolds in one endless set of mini-irritants.

You have an opportunity to speak to some non-Christian friends—a neighbor, someone over the back fence, someone at the gas station—and you are already in such a sour frame that when they ask some dumb question about religion, you answer with a kind of curtness and condescending wit that leaves them shriveled up in a pile of embarrassment. You feel guilty, but you have done it now. Eventually you return home, and your wife has cooked this disgusting stew that your children like and that you detest. You cannot be civil to her, and she cannot be civil to you. The kids that night are really not behaving particularly well. Your wife wants you to do jobs, and you want to watch football.

Finally it is time for bed at the end of this long day, and your prayer runs something like this: "Dear God, this has been a rotten day. I'm not very proud of myself; I'm frankly ashamed. But I really don't have anything to say. I'm sorry I have not done better. Forgive my sin. Bless everybody in the world. Your will be done. In Jesus' name, Amen."

But then a few days later you wake up to find the air is refreshingly cool. The sun is shining, the windows are open, the fresh air is wafting through the screen, and you hear the birds singing. You smell something delightful: "Bacon! I can't believe it! I wonder what the celebration is." You get up and reach for clean socks and feel full of energy. You're whistling as you wash in the bathroom and then have a wonderful quiet time with your spouse. You eat a hearty breakfast and then go out to your car, put the key in the ignition, and VROOM!—the car starts right up and takes off. You get to work early. Everybody commends your industriousness and intelligence in the way you discharge your duties. Your boss says, "Wonderful to see you today! Did I tell you that you are going to get a raise? You did such a great job on that contract."

Now you come across that same person at the gas station, and wonder of wonders the poor brute actually asks another question. This time, however, you respond with wisdom, tact, gentleness, understanding, courtesy, insight, and kindness. Lo and behold, he promises to come to church with you this coming Sunday. Then you arrive home, and there is a joyous family dinner. The kids are behaving, and you have intimate conversation with your wife while the two of you clean up the kitchen.

Finally, at the end of that day you get down to pray, and your prayer goes something like this: "Eternal and matchless God, we bow in your glorious presence with brokenness and gratitude. We bless you that in your infinite mercies and great grace you have poured favor upon us. We are not worthy of the least of your mercies . . ." And now you go on and on and on in flowery theological language. You thank God for all the things in the day, and then you pray for missionaries and their children and first cousins twice removed. Then you start praying for everyone you can think of in your church, and then you meditate on all the names of Christ that you can think of in Scripture. An hour goes by, and you go to bed and instantly fall asleep. Indeed, you go to sleep—justified.

On which of these two occasions have you fallen into the dreadful trap of paganism? God help us: the sad reality is that both approaches to God are abominations. How dare you approach the mercy-seat of God on the basis of what kind of day you had, as if that were the basis for our entrance into the presence of the sovereign and holy God? No wonder we cannot beat the Devil. This is works theology. It has nothing to do with grace and the exclusive sufficiency of Christ. Nothing.

Do you not understand that we overcome the accuser on the ground of the blood of Christ? Nothing more, nothing less. That is how we win. It is the only way we win. This is the only ground of our acceptance before God. That is why we can never get very far from the cross without distorting something fundamental, not only in doctrine but in elementary discipleship, faithful perseverance, obedience, and spiritual warfare against the enemy of our souls. If you drift far from the cross, you are done. You are defeated. We overcome the accuser of our brothers and sisters, we overcome our consciences, we overcome our bad tempers, we overcome our defeats, we overcome our lusts, we overcome our fears, we overcome our pettiness on the basis of the blood of the Lamb. We dare to approach a holy God praying in Jesus' name, appealing to the blood of the Lamb.

I need no other argument.
I need no other plea.
It is enough that Jesus died
And that he died for me.[1]

They overcame him by the word of their testimony (Rev. 12:11b).

In the opening chapter of the Bible, God speaks, and worlds leap into being. He sends forth his word, and it accomplishes whatever he sends it out to do. His supreme message is the Word incarnate. Servants in the church rule through the Word. In the world at large, the only offensive weapon we have, according to the symbolism in Ephesians 6, is the sword of the Spirit, which is the Word of God. So what do Christians do when they try to overcome the Devil and all his tricks in this wicked world? The Devil is working through politics, corruption, the media, the state, declining morals, secularism, pluralism, educational systems, and much more. How do Christians fight back? Do they form a political party? Do they picket the White House? Do they send a lot of letters to the prime minister? Can you imagine Paul setting up a circuit of letters to send off to Caesar?

Do not misunderstand me. We live in a democracy, which is a different form of government from Paul's, and our Christian responsibilities in this kind of context may mean that we should give a lot of thought as to how to be salt and light in a corrupt and corroding society. We dare not withdraw into a little holy huddle. *But* we must recognize with every ounce of our being that what finally transforms society is the gospel. There are responsibilities to legislate correctly and pass good laws; God loves justice and holds every nation to account for justice. Promote the well-being of the city. Of course we are responsible to look after the poor. *But* at the end of the day, what transforms society is still the gospel.

---

[1]Chorus to Lidie H. Edmunds's hymn "My Faith Has Found a Resting Place."

How does the gospel advance? By the word of our testimony: "They overcame him . . . by the word of their testimony" (Rev. 12:11). This does not mean that they gave their testimonies a lot. That may be a good thing to do, but that is not what this verse means. It refers to Christians bearing testimony to Christ; they bear witness to Christ. They gossip the gospel. They evangelize. That is the central way by which they bear witness to Christ.

There is no other way for the gospel to advance. You cannot see people converted by holding the sword to their throat. You cannot transform society by anything other than the proclamation of the gospel. What we *must* have is the promulgation and promotion of the gospel. Yet some of us have not shared the gospel with a single person in the last year or even five years. Even pastors fall into this trap as they retreat into a narrow little world where they talk only to other Christians. They have never made friends outside. They have no one with whom they can share the gospel completely, honestly, and generously. They do not talk about the gospel in the barber shop. They are afraid.

We overcome Satan on the ground of the blood of the cross, and we overcome also on the ground of this promulgated word. God has ordained that by the foolishness of the proclaimed message men and women will be saved.

It is not simply a question of how we survive the accusations of the Evil One. It is a question of how we fight the Evil One. We do so not by taking swords and becoming crusaders or by shooting the bad guys. We do so in the first instance by the proclamation of the gospel again and again and again. Thus, the kingdom of God advances by the power of the Spirit through the ministry of the Word. Not for a moment does that mitigate the importance of good deeds and understanding the social entailments of the gospel, but they are entailments *of the gospel*. It is *the gospel* that is preached. Thus, the only way that we can be defeated on this dimension is to be quiet. Our silence guarantees a measure of victory to Satan.

When was the last time you explained the gospel to an unbeliever one-on-one or one-on-three in a more-or-less neutral or even hostile environment? That is how the gospel advances. I know that conversion is finally a work of God. God can sweep through a population with great power and bring countless thousands into the kingdom in very short order. But normally the God of the Bible uses means. He has ordained that the gospel will advance by the foolishness of the Word preached, by bearing witness to Christ.

So when we look at our culture and observe, for example, rising polarities of worldview—one part still holding on to some of the residue of the Judeo-Christian heritage and other parts becoming more and more radicalized in philosophical materialism or in Eastern religions or in a dogmatic secular antithesis to Christianity—the first questions we ask should be these: How do we evangelize the people we do not like? How do we evangelize the people outside our heritage? How do we cross the barriers and evangelize people in the media or in another part of town or immigrants or Muslims? Do we evangelize only the people with whom we feel most comfortable? At the end of the day we overcome the Devil by bearing testimony to Jesus.

They overcame him by not loving their lives so much as to shrink from death (Rev. 12:11c).

They overcame Satan simply because they were willing to die.

Christians used to write books on how to die well. Their great prayer was that in their declining hours when their minds were going and they were no longer in control (but there were Christians who loved self-discipline) they would not say anything that would bring shame on the cross. Do you ever hear Christians pray like that today? Their prayer today is more likely to be, "Give me another shot of morphine so that I don't have to suffer."

"They did not love their lives so much as to shrink from death" (v. 11c). This is a rather different view of death from what drives many in the Western world. Suppose you belong to the official regime that decides to oppose the apostle Paul and the Christ whom he preaches. What are you going to do with Paul? Kill him? "For to me, to live is Christ," Paul writes—that is, it is living and promoting the gospel—"*and to die is gain*" (Phil. 1:21). It does not sound as if the threat of death will be a great deterrent to the apostle. We have been so relatively free in the West that we sometimes do not see what our brothers and sisters in Christ often face elsewhere. Those who compile the relevant statistics tell us that over the last ten years approximately 160,000 Christians a year have been martyred. It is easy to believe; there have been no fewer than two million martyrs alone, for example, in the southern Sudan during the last fifteen years or so. If 160,000 Christians continue to be martyred each year, it means that of all the Christians in the world today, one out of every two hundred will die a martyr's death. Now, of course, the martyrs are not evenly distributed across congregations, but would it not change our perspective a little bit if we saw it in those terms? Very few of us in the West are called upon to suffer like that—though there are rising cultural pressures that resort to mockery, ridicule, job pressures, and the like to keep Christians silent and ineffective. But there are many parts of the world where faithfulness to the gospel of Jesus Christ is, potentially, a matter of life and death.

Yet there is a broader principle at stake—a call to Christians to die to self-interest. All Christians must die to self. We are to take up our cross and follow Christ, and this means that by conscious act of the will strengthened by the Spirit, we choose to die to self-interest daily and promote Christ's interests daily. For that is not only an integral part of what it means to follow Jesus, but it is one of the three crucial steps to defeating the Devil. The Devil is still filled with fury, for he knows that his time is short. And Christians? "They did not love their lives so much as to shrink from death." How are you going to stop a movement the members of which, by God's sustaining grace, die to self-interest in order to serve the living God?

Conclusion

There are two applications of overwhelming importance.

1) Analyze culture biblically and theologically, not merely sociologically and psychologically.

In every generation we must analyze our situation biblically and theologically. I am certainly not saying that there is nothing to be learned about society from the surrounding disciplines. But we must understand that Revelation 12 gives us an analysis of the problems and challenges that the church faces that probes more deeply than the sociological, demographic, and historical dimensions to which we commonly first appeal. We need to understand and address those dimensions, too, of course, but Revelation 12 goes much deeper. It provides an analysis that is spiritual and cosmic in its sweep, and it provides the most fundamental of Christian responses. Martin Luther understood this very well. He taught us to sing:

> And though this world, with devils filled,
> Should threaten to undo us,
> We will not fear, for God hath willed
> His truth to triumph through us:

The Prince of Darkness grim,
We tremble not for him;
His rage we can endure,
For lo, his doom is sure,
One little word shall fell him.[2]

And that "little word" is the word of the gospel.

2) Use the weapons that Christ has provided, weapons based on Christ's atoning death.

These are the only effective weapons we have. Return to the cross and defeat the accuser of the brothers and sisters. Incessantly and in every venue bear witness to Christ, and defeat the accuser of the brothers and sisters. Retain courage and integrity in the face of opposition, because death cannot frighten those who follow the Prince of Life—and thereby defeat the accuser of the brothers and sisters.

Another song, "The Kingdom of Our God," attempts to capture the message of Revelation 12:

The enemy is fearsome;
His fury terrifies.
His arrogance is loathsome;
His foul mouth vilifies
The Son of God in heaven,
The angels he installed,
The offspring of the woman—
The people God has called.

Our foe has been defeated;
He knows his time is short,
And far from being seated

---

[2]Martin Luther, "A Mighty Fortress Is Our God," ca. 1529.

In honor in God's court,
His certain doom is looming
Like clouds before a squall,
And blind rage marks his booming
Attack upon us all.

He loves to foster warfare
Or peace with great deceit.
He aims to fill his death lair
With rebels; he repeats
His filthy accusations
To make us doubt the Lord;
He doles out tribulations
Of famine, plagues, and sword.

The father of all murder,
His passion is the lie;
In sin a tireless worker—
A tempter who will try
To dupe us with seduction,
Or persecute to death—
To challenge God's election,
Deny the Spirit's breath.

But we have overcome him by the blood of God's own Lamb.
We silence accusations; on Christ's death we take our stand.
The kingdom is advancing by the gospel we proclaim.
The truth to which we testify that frees from fear and shame.
We will not hide from danger, death, and other earthly loss,
For we are learning daily death, the pathway of the cross.
The devil fights with fury, with a cruel and
    bruising rod.
But we extol the triumph of the kingdom of our God.[3]

---

[3]D. A. Carson, "The Kingdom of Our God," track 2, in *Shout with Delight*, vol. 1 of New Songs for the People of God (1999).

Prayer

Forbid, Lord God, that we should rest so comfortably in our easy and restless society, that we forget that one of the driving dimensions of Christian experience is warfare—not against flesh and blood but against all the hosts of darkness who are filled with rage against us. Help us, Lord God, to see the enemy and then to deploy the gospel answers, the gospel arms, the gospel solutions, which alone are sufficient in this conflict. So return us to the cross, to faithful, glorious, grateful proclamation of the gospel, to self-death that we may follow the Lord Jesus, who died and rose on our behalf.

Again, Lord God, we ask that we not think too much of the Devil, for he is in principle a defeated foe, regardless of how vicious and how full of rage and how cruel he is. So we thank you for the triumph of the Lamb. Yet we would not think too little of him either, and thus leave ourselves unguarded. Protect our minds. Increase our self-discipline. Enlarge our ability to discern that the fundamental issues in any local church are not party politics—who's up and who's down, who's popular and who's not, what color the carpet is, whether someone's nose is out of joint. The Devil himself is a roaring lion seeking whom he may devour, yet he often moves subtly, deceiving if it were possible the very elect. So lead us not into temptation, but deliver us from the evil one. For yours is the kingdom and the power and the glory forever. Amen.

On his arrival, Jesus found that Lazarus had already been in the tomb for four days. Bethany was less than two miles from Jerusalem, and many Jews had come to Martha and Mary to comfort them in the loss of their brother. When Martha heard that Jesus was coming, she went out to meet him, but Mary stayed at home.

"Lord," Martha said to Jesus, "if you had been here, my brother would not have died. But I know that even now God will give you whatever you ask."

Jesus said to her, "Your brother will rise again."

Martha answered, "I know he will rise again in the resurrection at the last day."

Jesus said to her, "I am the resurrection and the life. Anyone who believes in me will live, even though he dies and whoever believes in me will never die. Do you believe this?"

"Yes, Lord," she told him, "I believe that you are the Christ, the Son of God, who was to come into the world."

—JOHN 11:17–27

4
A Miracle Full of Surprises

John 11:1–53

So often God surprises us.

Moses thought so: endless years on the backside of a desert; now eighty years of age; his own family—children, grandchildren—passed by for any redemptive purpose for the nation; suffering a speech defect; and an outsider now to the courts of Egypt. Yet at the age of eighty he was called by God to lead the covenant people out of the land of slavery and to become the mediator of a covenant that would shape their lives for millennia. It was more than a little surprising. But so often God is surprising.

Habakkuk thought so. It was all right for God to use wicked nations to punish other nations that were still more wicked. The prophet could understand that. But for God to use the pagan powers all around Israel to punish Israel, God's covenant people, who on any showing were less steeped in social pathology than Assyria or Babylon, that was a bit much. But God surprises us.

Paul thought so. He had prayed for others to be healed, and he had seen some of those prayers answered. He then prayed for himself when he suffered his own thorn in the flesh—three times in long intercession—and God's only answer was, "My grace is sufficient for you, for my power is made perfect in weakness" (2 Cor. 12:9). Initially Paul found that answer inadequate, and more than a little surprising.

There are many more witnesses that could be called upon. This is a truth not to be passed over lightly: God often surprises us; he is not to be domesticated by reductionistic theology; he takes the common things and turns them into surprising things. That is why large swaths of the Bible are written with various kinds of twist: you think you know where the words are going, and then the text jumps in another direction. Could anyone have predicted how the story of Job would turn out? Or how Habakkuk would turn out?

One of the New Testament writers most given to surprise is John. Because many of us have become superficially familiar with the Bible, we sometimes miss these surprising elements. They no longer surprise us because we have read the text before. That is one of the reasons why we do well to think through, as far as we are able, how these texts would have been understood by their first readers when they were first read aloud.

Most chapters in John preserve some sort of surprising note, but none more so than John 11, the account of the raising of Lazarus from the dead, the chapter where Jesus makes this remarkable claim: "I am the resurrection and the life" (v. 25). If we are to understand that claim correctly and how it bears on us today, we will be better positioned to do so if we take the time to see how it is embedded in unfolding surprise.

It will be convenient to divide the text into four points, each steeped in surprise.

Jesus Receives a Desperate Plea for Help and Demonstrates His Love by Delay (John 11:1–16)

The account begins with a request for help from Mary and Martha regarding their brother Lazarus. In the original manuscript, of course, there was no chapter division at this point, so you would have read on from the end of chapter 10, which places Jesus at a particular point. He is at "the place where John had been baptizing in the early days" (v. 40). That takes you back to chapter 1, to a place that our English translations call Bethany, which is actually Batanea (Βηθανία; *Bēthania*). Batanea is up in the Galilee district. Lazarus lies ill in Bethany of Judea, which is a little less than two miles from Jerusalem, just on the other side of the slopes of the Mount of Olives. The places are separated by about 110 miles.

Clearly Jesus loved this family. Lazarus's sisters refer to their brother as "the one you love" (11:3), an expression that hints of all kinds of human relationships that Jesus had of which we know rather little. I do think, though, that it is one of the common features of those who become intimate with Jesus that they think of themselves not as those who love him particularly well but those who are particularly well loved by him. Thus, John, the writer of this Gospel, refers to himself as "the disciple whom Jesus loved" (13:23; 21:7, 20; cf. 20:2). Or Paul, referring to Jesus in an atonement passage, adds the clause "who loved me and gave himself for me" (Gal. 2:20). Paul prays that the Ephesians "may have power, together with all the saints, to grasp how wide and long and high and deep is the love of Christ, and to know this love that surpasses knowledge" (Eph. 3:18–19a). Those who draw really close to Jesus think of themselves, first and foremost, as those loved by him rather than as those who profess their love for him.

At the same time, doubtless the sisters were trying to play on Jesus' emotions: "The one you love is sick" (John 11:3). They invite him to demonstrate his love by doing something about this illness.

"When he heard this, Jesus said [to his disciples], 'This sickness will not end in death. No, it is for God's glory so that God's Son may be glorified through it'" (v. 4). At one level, of course, this illness does lead to death—but it does not *end* in death, as Jesus puts it. In the storyline of the narrative, it *ends* in resurrection. But perhaps Jesus is using "end" in a punning way: the event's *purpose*, its true and ultimate *end*, is not death, or even the resurrection of Lazarus, but God's display of his glory, that is, so that God's Son may be glorified through it. As usual in John, Jesus' *miracles* are called "signs": they point beyond themselves to something else. They are *sign*ificant. The first sign, changing water into wine, ends with this statement: "This, the first of his miraculous signs, Jesus performed in Cana of Galilee. He thus *revealed his glory*, and his disciples put their faith in him" (2:11). So now this illness too is fitting into a larger pattern in which God will display his glory, in Jesus, again. Before this miracle is over, it will have served as a *sign*post to Jesus' own death and resurrection.

But we are getting ahead of ourselves (as John himself often does: he tantalizes his readers with bits and pieces, with surprising expressions that make sense only later in his narrative). John has established that Jesus loved Lazarus and that Lazarus's illness has as its "end" the glory of God in the glorification of Jesus. How this is to be worked out is not yet clear. Then John returns to Jesus' love. We read, "Now Jesus loved Martha and her sister and Lazarus" (11:5). There is that close relationship again. So what we might expect as the next line is something like this: "So because of his love, as soon as Jesus received word of Lazarus's illness, he collected his disciples and immediately headed south as fast as his legs could carry him." But instead we read, "*So* when he heard that Lazarus was sick, he stayed where he was two more days." What kind of logic is that? Jesus receives a desperate plea for help and demonstrates his love—by delay! The flow is so surprising that the NIV translates verse 6 with the word "yet": "*Yet* when he heard that Lazarus was sick, he stayed where he was two more days." But "*so*" is the right word; indeed, the original could be taken even more strongly: "Jesus loved Martha and her sister and Lazarus. *Therefore*, when he heard that Lazarus was sick, he stayed where he was two more days" (vv. 5–6). On an initial reading, verse 6 is almost scandalous.

But the surprise is not yet over. John tells us that Jesus remains where he is for two days and then says, "Let us go back to Judea" (v. 7). Remember those two days: they are setting us up for the next surprise. The disciples are not pleased that he is going back to Judea at all because all along Jesus faces greater threats of violent opposition in the south, in Judea, than in the north, in Galilee (v. 8). But Jesus replies with a little parable:

> Jesus answered, "Are there not twelve hours of daylight? A man who walks by day will not stumble, for he sees by this world's light. It is when he walks by night that he stumbles, for he has no light."
> (vv. 9–10)

Jesus means that by his returning to the south he is doing the will of God; he is walking in the light. So if you walk in the light, you cannot stumble. You cannot be wrong if you follow the will of God. Not to do God's will is the equivalent of walking at night, in the darkness, when you are far more likely to stumble. This little parable would speak powerfully in a culture without electric lights: the night could really be dark, the way intrinsically dangerous.

But now, at the end of the two-day delay, Jesus says, "Our friend Lazarus has fallen asleep; but I am going there to wake him up" (v. 11). At this point he declares that Lazarus is not only sick but dead. How he knows this is simply part of his reliance upon his Father for supernatural information. He knows things that humans normally do not. There is no telephone or radio, no satellite to make instantaneous communication possible. From Batanea in the north to Bethany in the south is about 110 miles, a three-to-four-days' walking journey for a fit man. So he receives news of Lazarus's illness, waits two days, and then decides to leave once he knows that Lazarus is dead.

His disciples misunderstand his metaphor of sleep: "Lord, if he sleeps, he will get better," they say, thinking perhaps that the fever has broken (v. 12). But "Jesus had been speaking of his death'" (v. 13a). "So then he told them plainly, 'Lazarus is dead, and *for your sake I am glad I was not there, so that you may believe.* But let us go to him'" (vv. 14–15). In other words, his being absent meant that Lazarus would die; if he had been there, doubtless, precisely because Jesus did love him, he would have healed him while he was merely ill. And in that case the forthcoming miracle reported in this chapter would never have occurred. Its particular "end" in bringing glory to God by glorifying Jesus would never have taken place.

Still, why the delay? He waited *two* days. "On his arrival, Jesus found that Lazarus had already been in the tomb for *four* days" (v. 17). Martha later says to Jesus, "Lord . . . by this time there is a bad odor, for he has been there *four* days" (v. 39). If Jesus had set out as soon as he received the report of Lazarus's illness and come south, Lazarus still would have been dead by the time that Jesus arrived, and Jesus still could have performed the miracle. In that case, of course, Lazarus would have been dead for only two days. Still, dead is dead. If Jesus had responded immediately, at very least his promptness would have relieved Mary and Martha of two days of bereavement, would it not? So why bother delaying? Why John's insistence that Jesus' delay was the result of his love for Mary, Martha, and Lazarus (vv. 5–6)?

The delay turns on something that is a little strange to most Western societies but would have been easily understood in the first century. In fact, it would have been understood even in much of the Western world until a hundred or a hundred and fifty years ago. There was a Jewish superstition that when you die, your spirit hovers over you for up to three days and then departs. At that point no resuscitation is possible. Thus, you read in a Rabbinical commentary (*Lev. Rab.* 18:1) that the soul hovers over the body of the deceased person for the first three days "intending to re-enter it, but as soon as it sees its appearance change," that is, as soon as decomposition has set in, it departs. Death is then judged irreversible.

One suspects that the reason such superstitions grew up is pretty obvious to any culture that does not handle bodies the way we handle them today. Today when someone dies the body is immediately whisked out to the mortuary where it disappears from public view for a day or two. It is embalmed, made to look as lifelike as possible, and then laid out in an open casket for a viewing. There are relatively few people today in the Western world who are buried without first being embalmed in some measure. But that is a fairly recent innovation.

When my grandfather died in a poor London home in 1919, he was laid out in an inexpensive casket on the kitchen table. People viewed him on that first day, and he was buried within twenty-four hours. That was not uncommon. Indeed, such speed is mandated in much of the Muslim world today. Of course, if there was both speed and an absence of competent medical attention, it was quite possible for someone to be judged dead when the person thought to be deceased was actually still alive. Perhaps the patient's heart was merely fibrillating, and no pulse could be felt; perhaps the patient was scarcely breathing. And then as the people gathered for the funeral and carried the casket out to the burial ground, the patient might wake up and knock on the wooden box. There are not a few accounts of this sort in the literature. In fact, I was explaining this passage on one occasion in England, and an elderly lady came up to me afterwards and said, "That's exactly what happened to my grandfather.

We were actually carrying him on our shoulders to the church burial plot when we heard a knock on the wood from inside the casket."

It is understandable, then, how a certain tradition would develop to the effect that the spirit hangs on in the area for a while and then after the face has changed, that is, after such decomposition has occurred no reversal is possible, the spirit departs. I am not suggesting for a moment that Jesus holds that particular superstition. But if Jesus had arrived two days earlier and brought Lazarus back from the dead, some would have said, "Aha, yes. We know how this one works."

In fact, during the first and second centuries, certain astute healers manipulated people through the ambiguity of death's timing. For example, Apollonius of Tyana pulled back from the dead two or three people, and it was openly said that he was the kind of doctor who had special powers to see when there were still vital signs left. He would use a draft of wine and herbs and secret ingredients so as to stimulate them again. People were not quite sure whether it was a resurrection or some really insightful cure. You can read the document to this day; it has been translated into English.

But with Jesus staying away those extra two days, the miracle he performed took place on the fourth day—a point that is repeated—and so long after Lazarus's death that decomposition had set in. That is the point of verse 39: Martha protests when Jesus wants the tomb opened, for "by this time there is a bad odor, for he has been there four days." The point is that there is no way you can doubt that Lazarus was dead. He was dead to the point of decay. There was no embalming. And in that kind of heat, decay would set in. The man was dead.

When in those days people from wealthier homes wrapped a corpse in strips of cloth and enclosed ointments in these cloths (as Joseph of Arimathea did with Jesus), it was not primarily to embalm and to preserve. It was simply to quell the smell. These were not embalming perfumes. They were simply smell-quenching perfumes.

In short, by his delay Jesus demonstrates his love by guaranteeing that when he arrives there, not only is Lazarus dead (which he would have been even if Jesus had set out immediately), but that he has been dead such a long time that when he performs the miracle, it is deeply *sign*ificant. While they were waiting for Jesus' arrival, of course, Mary did not know that, and Martha did not know that. But God works in surprising ways, and sometimes he demonstrates his love by delay.

Little children understand very little about time beyond the *now*. Teaching a three-year-old the pleasure of deferred gratification is almost impossible. That is why all of us recognize that it is the little child who wants something immediately, not in some ambiguous and uncertain future, who cries, "Now! Now! Now!" Sadly, many of us act like very young and immature children when we deal with God. We, too, want specific blessings *now, now, now*. But God takes the long view, and he understands that sometimes delay is what is best for us. Think of this passage from Romans 5:3–5:

> Not only so, but we also rejoice in our sufferings, because we know that suffering produces perseverance; perseverance, character; and character, hope. And hope does not disappoint us, because God has poured out his love into our hearts by the Holy Spirit, whom he has given to us.

You get the impression from this passage that both Paul and God share this vision that the development of character, perseverance, and eschatological hope are more important than simply relief from suffering.

That is not something that the West knows much about. We expect God simply to release us immediately (if not sooner!) or jolly well give us an explanation. But God may be less interested in giving us explanations than in building character.

A friend of mine who was a pastor of a church was shaking hands at the door a number of years ago. A woman shook his hand and said, "Pastor, pray for me that I might be given more patience."

He replied, "I will pray that the Lord will send you a packet of trouble."

She said, "That is exactly what I don't need. I've already got trouble. All I need is patience."

"Well, if you want patience, I'll pray that the Lord will give you a packet of trouble"—because that is the way the Lord regularly does things.

Suffering produces perseverance, which produces the character. God normally uses means.

I first arrived in Chicago to join the faculty of Trinity Evangelical Divinity School in 1978. In the spring of 1979, a rather remarkable event happened at Trinity. Even then it was a school of one thousand or so, and to avoid endless adjustment of exam schedules, we have some pretty firm rules in place, rules that prescribe when you must take those exams. If the exam for your course is set for a certain time and place, you take it at that time and place—no exceptions (unless, of course, your spouse dies or you hear that your father has had a heart attack, or something of that order). If you think that you have a sufficiently strong reason to reschedule your exam, you must clear the rescheduling with the dean of students in advance. Valid reasons are posted; students are clearly told that other requests will not be accommodated.

In the spring of 1979, one particular couple was planning on leaving early for a weekend engagement in California—an engagement at a church that was interested in inviting the man to join their pastoral staff.

This church wanted them to arrive on Friday afternoon—early evening at latest—so that they could spend a little extra time with the church. So without telling this church that they had final exams slated for that Friday afternoon, this couple said, "Sure, that's fine." Without telling the Trinity administration, they booked their passage and only then approached the dean of students, doubtless thinking that the fact that they had already booked the passage would give them leverage.

Trinity remained unpersuaded by the urgency of this request, and the student said, "But aren't you really interested in ministry? We are going out to minister. This is a call to a church. This surely takes priority."

"But you understood the rules in advance."

"But this is going to cost us money. We cannot change these tickets. These are special weekend tickets."

"You understood the rules before you signed up. You didn't ask us first. You did this knowing that you were acting outside the stipulated policy of the Divinity School."

This couple was really disgruntled. They badmouthed the seminary endlessly for two weeks. Faculty and administration were nothing but dry-as-dust academics who were not interested in ministry. They were still mumbling after the exam on the Friday afternoon when they came into the Whitehorse Inn, a little coffee shop. The radio was on, and a newsflash was being broadcast: a plane had crashed at Chicago's O'Hare Airport and killed everyone on board. That was the Chicago crash of '79. It was the flight they had booked to California.

Not for a moment am I suggesting that all Christians are spared coming down in airplane crashes. On the other hand, God is in charge of that, too. It made this couple reflect a little more on their urgency, their passion to do what they wanted regardless of what arrangements had been made, on their urge to succeed and press ahead, on the bitterness of their own responses. And inevitably it made them reflect a little on the mysteries of providence.

God is sovereign. He is wise. He is unqualifiedly good. Part of Christian maturation is understanding that even his delays are not foolish or stupid or mistakes or exercises in whimsy. He is to be trusted, and even the delays are to be improved upon by the way we respond to them.

> Ye fearful saints, fresh courage take,
> The clouds ye so much dread
> Are big with mercy, and shall break
> In blessings on your head.
>
> Judge not the Lord by feeble sense,
> But trust Him for His grace;
> Behind a frowning providence
> He hides a smiling face.
>
> His purposes will ripen fast,
> Unfolding every hour;
> The bud may have a bitter taste,
> But sweet will be the flower.
>
> Blind unbelief is sure to err,
> And scan his work in vain;
> God is His own interpreter,
> And He will make it plain.[1]

So here is the first surprise: Jesus receives a desperate plea for help and demonstrates his love—by delay.

---

[1] William Cowper (1731–1800), "God Works in a Mysterious Way," 1774.

Jesus Comes Up Against Devastating Loss and Consoles Grief by Directing Attention to Himself (John 11:17–27)

"On his arrival, Jesus found that Lazarus had already been in the tomb for four days" (v. 17). Already John is preparing the ground for this four-day delay. "Bethany was less than two miles from Jerusalem, and many Jews had come [from Jerusalem] to Martha and Mary to comfort them in the loss of their brother" (vv. 18–19). These Jews had come out of the city to console Lazarus's family, who were village people but quite posh. They had large bank accounts and a lot of contacts. This family had enough money to expend an entire jar of ointment on Jesus when that jar cost about a year's salary for a day laborer: perhaps $25,000 or $30,000 in today's currency (12:1ff.). It is not surprising that many people from the city of Jerusalem came out to console them in their loss.

When Martha hears that Jesus is coming, she slips out of the house to try to meet him privately on the road. Hence the dialog beginning in verse 21: "Lord," Martha said to Jesus, "if you had been here, my brother would not have died." This is probably not a rebuke. She is probably not saying, "Lord, it's all your fault! If only you had been here!" That is a harsh reading. It is more likely a lament expressing anguish, realizing that it could have been another way. If Jesus had been there, he would have healed her brother, and Lazarus would not have died. It is a broken "Oh, if only . . ." lament.

Then it is almost as if Martha overhears her own statement and perceives what it sounds like: it sounds as if she is blaming Jesus, as if Lazarus's death is his fault. So she quickly adds, "But I know that even now God will give you whatever you ask" (v. 22). This does not mean that Martha now understands that a resurrection is about to take place. The whole narrative shows that she does not expect it (see esp. 11:39).

It is merely a polite acknowledgment that Jesus is powerful. She is not blaming him. She knows that even now Jesus can ask his Father and that his Father will do wonderful things through him.

"Jesus said to her, 'Your brother will rise again'" (v. 23). Martha is orthodox. She knows, as do Pharisees and Christians but not Sadducees, that there is a resurrection at the last day. So she hears Jesus to be saying no more than this: "Lazarus is dead, but death does not have the last word. He will rise again on the last day." To this she replies, "I know he will rise again in the resurrection at the last day" (v. 24). She has no expectation that Jesus will raise Lazarus now.

But then Jesus introduces a twist into the conversation that turns attention away from Lazarus and Martha, away from his death and her bereavement. Almost scandalously, he turns attention to himself: "Jesus said to her, 'I am the resurrection and the life. He who believes in me will live, even though he dies; and whoever lives and believes in me will never die. Do you believe this?'" (vv. 25–26). Remarkably, Jesus focuses attention away from a generalized belief as to what takes place on the last day, and toward himself. He is not offering the comfort of saying, "Yes, my dear sister, there is a resurrection on the last day." He is saying, "I want you to believe something more than that. I *am* the resurrection and the life." What does he mean by this?

In fact, Jesus is making two claims that are intertwined—and then he unpacks both of them.

1) *"I am the resurrection"*: Where there is death, Jesus resurrects people. And then the explanation: "He who believes in me will live, even though he dies" (v. 25). "He who believes in me" (trusts in Jesus) will come to life again on the other side of death. Death is not the final word. The one who dies will live. There is resurrection beyond death.

2) *"I am the life"*: Jesus gives eternal life. "Whoever lives and believes

in me will never die." One gains eternal life *now*, and the believer who gains such eternal life will never die, will never lose that eternal life. That life goes on and on and on and on. That believer may yet pass through physical death, but Jesus is the life, and those who believe in him will never die.

Nevertheless, Jesus' claim, "I am the resurrection and the life," is not transparent. True, we can see how he *gives* resurrection and life, but what does he mean by claiming to *be* resurrection and life? An illustration may help. Some with longer memories may recall the time when Kentucky Fried Chicken first appeared on the market. Everywhere you looked you were presented with this white-headed, white-goateed man in advertisements on billboards, television, and radio. He claimed that his chicken was cooked in a recipe of eleven secret herbs, and that it was "finger-lickin' good." This so caught the market at the time that it would have been quite conceivable for Colonel Sanders with his famous Kentucky Fried finger-lickin' good Chicken to say something like this: "I *am* Kentucky Fried Chicken." Everyone would have understood what he meant. He would not have been making an ontological claim: "I am a chicken from Kentucky, fried or otherwise. Cluck-cluck, cluck-cluck." Everyone would have understood that he meant something like this: "I am so identified with Kentucky Fried Chicken that apart from me there is no Kentucky Fried Chicken. There are surrogates and placebos and fake claims, but if you really want Kentucky Fried finger-lickin' good Chicken, you must get my chicken. I am identified with this chicken, and no one else can provide it. I *am* Kentucky Fried Chicken."

Another example: Charles de Gaulle said on more than one occasion, "I am the state." At some ontological level, the claim was nonsensical. After all, de Gaulle has now gone, and the state of France is still there. But in the troubled period after the third republic, de Gaulle alone held the fabric of the nation together and prevented it from sliding into near anarchy or worse. So it is understandable that a man with his ego should say, "I am the state" and mean in effect, "Apart from me, at the moment, there is no France."

What Jesus says when he claims, "I am the resurrection and the life," is the same kind of utterance, but without a hint of bravado or arrogance. What he is stating is not an ontological claim. He simply means, "So exclusively am I the provider of resurrection and eternal life that apart from me there is no resurrection and life."

So Jesus is now encouraging Martha, who has been prepared to confess her belief in the final resurrection at the last day, to believe something more: not only that there is final resurrection at the last day, but that the only one who can provide it is the one who says, "I am the resurrection and the life." The only one who can provide eternal life is this Jesus. That is his claim. "Martha, do you believe this?"

Imagine! In the midst of her mourning and loss, when she is in the bog of despair, Jesus preaches a sermon about himself. He is not asking if she believes that he is about to raise her brother from the dead immediately, but if her faith that there will be a resurrection at the end can extend to deep trust in Jesus himself as the one who grants eternal life now and will resurrect the dead on the last day. In short, he asks her if she can trust him as the resurrection and the life. He diverts attention from her grief to his own transcendent claims. If she answers positively, then the raising of Lazarus itself becomes a kind of acted parable of the life-giving power of Jesus. And she replies, "Yes, Lord, I believe that you are the Messiah, the Son of God, who was to come into the world" (v. 27).

Her reply carries the narrative forward, for clearly she believes that the one who is the resurrection and the life must be such by virtue of the fact that he is the Messiah. She still does not believe that he is going to do anything with her brother at the moment (cf. v. 39).

Nevertheless this is a remarkable exchange. Jesus butts up against devastating loss and offers comfort—by diverting attention to himself. I am not for a moment suggesting that there is no place in our consoling of those who are bereaved for simply listening, weeping, holding a hand, helping with the gardening, or preparing a meal. But among genuine believers, the greatest consolation of all comes from focusing on Christ. Not even the raw creedal points of faith are sufficient, as important as they are. For example, "You will see your brother again: there is a general resurrection at the end of the age." That is true, and Martha believed it; but it did not help much. What Jesus does is divert attention to himself. Believers will understand that this is spectacularly encouraging and glorious; others will interpret Jesus' approach as scandalously egocentric.

A friend of mine—another pastor I knew rather well some years ago—tells of a young man in his congregation who was powerfully converted out of a really rocky background. Within a very short time (months at most), he was diagnosed as having a vicious melanoma that left him with only weeks to live. His family had written him off, and he was an ex-junkie with no friends except for this group of Christians who had borne witness to him and who had seen his conversion. When the Christians went to visit him in the hospital, they were understandably nervous. They thought, "How is this chap's faith going to stand up now? No sooner does he become a Christian than he is struck down with cancer." As his body began to bloat and his face began to waste away, they would go in with more and more fear and trepidation until it became clear that what he wanted from them when they came in was for them to read John 11 and 1 Corinthians 15, pray with him, and talk about the love of Christ.

In our deepest loss, we need more than friendship and a listening ear—though they are wonderful. We need more than mere arguments—though in some cases good arguments stabilize us. We need the reality of God himself—God as he has spectacularly and definitively disclosed himself to us in the person of his Son. He will require of us that we focus our attention on him, both for this life and the one to come.

Jesus Confronts Implacable Death and Displays His Sovereignty Over It in Tears and Outrage (John 11:28–44)

This third surprising turn in the narrative discloses itself in the context of Jesus' interview with Mary, Martha's sister. Apparently Martha returns home and tells Mary that the Teacher is nearby, wanting to meet her (v. 29). Mary gets up quickly and heads out, planning to meet Jesus. This interview turns out rather differently from the one with Martha, however, because this time the crowd spots Mary leaving and supposes she is going to the tomb to mourn. In those days the cultural patterns of grief were very different from what we go through today. Today it is considered good form to weep discretely, dab tears and turn away, to be quiet and subdued. We go into a mortuary, and our voices go down to a whisper as we talk quietly. We might well consider it good taste to let the bereaved family member go to the tomb in peace and privacy. But in many cultures in the world, including the Jewish culture in the first century, that was simply not the way it was. They expressed grief with loud cries and wails, often communally. You can still see something similar in various immigrant groups today: witness many Greek Orthodox and Muslim funerals, for instance. In the first century, not only did the mourners themselves wail, but they hired professional mourners to keep the noise and tears flowing. In fact, it was customary for even the poorest family to hire a minimum of two flute players and a professional wailing woman (Mishnah *Ketubbot* 4:4). The flute players would play dirges in minor keys to increase the solemnity and sadness of the occasion, and the professional wailing woman would increase the volume level every time it lowered.

Lazarus's family was not a poor one. This was a posh family with lots of money. Who knows how many musicians they hired? Certainly there was a lot of noise. John tells us that when they see Mary slipping away, they think that she is going off to the tomb, and they think, "We'll follow along to provide her with the appropriate support."

So a great number of people from Jerusalem are there following Mary, along with the intimates from the village of Bethany. But Mary does not go to the tomb. She heads up the road to find Jesus and approaches him with exactly the same words that Martha used: "Lord, if you had been here, my brother would not have died" (John 11:32).

But this time round the conversation takes a very different turn. Who knows where it might have gone if the crowd had not been there? Perhaps Jesus' conversation with Mary would have followed a line very similar to what ensued with Martha. But "when Jesus saw her weeping, and the Jews who had come along with her also weeping"—this is noisy now; not quietly-dab-your-tears but first-class noise—"he was *deeply moved* in spirit and troubled." There is no way that the original text should be rendered that way. I hate to mention two translation mistakes in one passage, but this is just a plain flat-out mistake in translation. It means "he was outraged" (not "deeply moved"). That is what this verb always means whenever it is applied to human beings. Interestingly, all the German translations I've checked have it right; all the English ones I've checked have it wrong. (That fact, I suppose, shows how often there is a controlling tradition even in our Bible translation.)

"'Where have you laid him?' he asked. 'Come and see, Lord,' they replied. Jesus wept" (vv. 34–35). Probably the fact that Jesus wept is what has constrained some people to render the earlier verb "he was deeply moved." but that is simply not what it means. Jesus was outraged? But why? And why did he weep? Why these responses? They seem so surprising.

It surely was not because he was powerless and frustrated. He was only minutes from one of his most spectacular miracles. Nor is it that he feels forced into doing a miracle (although some commentators have suggested this slightly bizarre notion). This was the very reason he came down south to Bethany. Nor is it simply that he misses his friend Lazarus, as if Jesus' tears at the loss of Lazarus are essentially analogous to our tears at the loss of a loved one. It is impudent to try to put yourself in Jesus' place, but so far as you can, do so in this instance. If you are crying because your friend has died when you know full well that you are going to raise him from the dead in about two minutes, how genuine would the tears be?

It is important to keep reminding ourselves of the context. Jesus sees all these people weeping, crying, and wailing in the face of implacable death, and he is outraged. He is profoundly troubled, so emotionally worked up over it that he weeps. There is a compassion in these tears, but there is also outrage. Jesus is outraged not because he has lost a friend but because of death itself. Death is such an ugly enemy. It generates endless and incalculable anguish. And for anyone steeped in the entire biblical heritage, death itself is a mark of sin.

How is death introduced to the race? Death itself is nothing other than God's insistence that human hubris will go so far and no farther. It is God's judicial response to our warped rebellion. Whether death afflicts us at five or ten or thirty or fifty or seventy or eighty years, it comes, and it is implacable. We are sinners, and we will die. Every time there is death, it still hurts. It is still painful. It is still ugly. And it is still the result of sin. This was not the way God made the creation in the first place. Jesus is outraged by the whole thing. He is outraged by the death that has called forth this loss, by the sin that lies behind that, and by the unbelief that characterizes everyone's response to it. There is outrage, and there is grief.

Christians must adopt something of this same stance toward death. There is a school of thought in Christian circles that almost views death so much as a blessing that you are not allowed to cry. Inevitably you meet some well-meaning types who will come up to you when you have just lost a spouse or a parent or a child, put their arms around you, and say, "To be absent from the body is to be present with the Lord." This can come from a mature believer who has surrounded you with support and understanding, and his quotation from the Bible sounds like a word from the Lord. But it can also come from someone who has never experienced the debilitation of terrible grief, and then the same quotation can sound like empty words or even spiritual one-upmanship. And you basically want to kick him. Then you feel guilty for wanting to kick him because you have let down the side. So why do you feel so angry?

The Bible is more brutally realistic. It dares to recognize death as the last enemy. Death *is* an enemy, and it can be a fierce one. Death is not normal when you look at it from the vantage point of what God created in the first place. It is normal this side of the fall, but that is not saying much. It is an enemy. It is ugly. It destroys relationships. It is to be feared. It is repulsive. There is something odious about death. Never ever pretend otherwise. But death does not have the last word. It is the last enemy, but more to be feared yet is the second death. Thank God for a Savior who could claim, "I am the resurrection and the life." Thus when we come to grips with these things, there needs to be both outrage and pain on the one hand and trust and quiet confidence on the other. The appropriate mingling of these things together is part of a genuinely Christian response to the ugliness, shock, terror, and loss of death. We begin to understand, and we sorrow, but not as those who have no hope.

When Jesus looks at the crowd of mourners, there is both outrage and tears. Tears without outrage quickly degenerate into mere sentimentality. Outrage without tears hardens into arrogance and bad-temper irascibility and unbelief. But Jesus displays both. He begins to display his divine sovereignty over death—by tears and outrage.

"Then the Jews said, 'See how he loved him!' But some of them said, 'Could not he who opened the eyes of the blind man have kept this man from dying?'" (vv. 36–37). The Jews were right and wrong in both of their responses.

Yes, Jesus loved Lazarus. He loved him so much that he returned to Judea where the political climate was so much more dangerous than in the north. It was a fateful decision that would take him to the cross. But the crowds were nevertheless wrong in this assessment because they drew their conclusion from Jesus' tears, without (as we have seen) really understanding those tears.

Yes, Jesus could have kept Lazarus from dying. But then again, he could not have done so if he was going to do the Father's will and bring about this miracle that would more greatly display the Father's glory in the glorification of Jesus.

Superficial reactions. No real understanding.

"Jesus, once more deeply moved, came to the tomb. It was a cave with a stone laid across the entrance" (v. 38). "Deeply moved" is that same verb again that should be translated "outraged": as Jesus comes to the tomb, once more he is frankly outraged.

"'Take away the stone,' he said" (v. 39a).

"But, Lord," Martha protests, "'by this time there is a bad odor, for he has been there four days.' Then Jesus said, 'Did I not tell you that if you believed, you will see the glory of God?'" (vv. 39b–40).

"So they took away the stone" (v. 41a). Now Jesus prays, but John reminds his readers that this prayer of Jesus is a public prayer—and so Jesus wants people to learn something from it. Prayers in public have not only God as the ultimate hearer but also other people, people who are listening in. Though still a prayer to God, the prayer has a pedagogical function. So Jesus crafts his prayer along those lines:

> "Father, I thank you that you have heard me. I knew that you always hear me, but I said this for the benefit of the people standing here, that they may believe that you sent me."
>
> When he had said this, Jesus called in a loud voice, "Lazarus, come out!" The dead man came out, his hands and feet wrapped with strips of linen, and a cloth around his face. Jesus said to them, "Take off the grave clothes and let him go." (vv. 41b–44)

Some wag has said that if Jesus had not stipulated "Lazarus," all the graves in Jerusalem would have opened. At one level that is fanciful. At another level it is exactly right because on the last day, Jesus is the one who will say, "Come forth!" And they really will come forth. My father will come forth. Adolf Hitler will come forth. The friend I lost when I was twelve will come forth. Some will come forth to the resurrection of life and some to the resurrection of death (John 5:21–29). The one who cried, "Lazarus, come out!" will cry again, and the graves will open.

The focus of the narrative thus rightly remains on Jesus Christ, not on Lazarus. The writer does not tell us a single thing about what Lazarus experienced during those four days. Nor does he inform us how Lazarus died (again!). For Lazarus was raised from the dead in the mortal, bodily form he had before this experience—quite unlike the resurrection of

Jesus. Like Lazarus, Jesus, too, was raised from the dead, and his tomb was as empty as that of Lazarus—but Jesus was raised (as we shall see in the next chapter) with an utterly transformed body that could never taste death again, a resurrection body peculiarly suited to the glories of the new heaven and the new earth still to come, a resurrection body that anticipates what all of Christ's redeemed people will one day enjoy. What Lazarus knew is simply not told. The silence is stunning, a silence nowhere more powerfully summarized than in four lines by the English poet Alfred Lord Tennyson:

> Behold a man raised up by Christ:
>> The rest remaineth unrevealed;
>> He told it not; or something seal'd
> The lips of the Evangelist.

But what John *does* tell is of incalculably greater importance. Christ displays his sovereignty over death, daring to reverse it. Yet this is no mere display of irresistible power. It is more than that. It is the display of Jesus' sovereignty over death *within the context of tears and outrage.* This sovereign Lord, so utterly powerful, so amazingly surprising, is personally engaged in the redemption of his broken, rebellious, image bearers.

Jesus Comes Up Against Moral and Spiritual Death and Gives Life by Dying Himself (John 11:45–53)

The plot to murder Jesus contains two profound surprises:

First, the Jewish religious leaders plot to murder Jesus in order to preserve their place—their temple and their nation—yet within forty years, the Romans destroy both.

Many of the Jews witness this astonishing miracle of the raising of Lazarus and put their faith in Jesus (v. 45), but it is hard to be sure how real their faith is. Some of them, however, simply go and rat to the Pharisees (v. 46), seeing one more opportunity to get in on the inside track with the religious and political authorities.

"Then the chief priests and the Pharisees called a meeting of the Sanhedrin. 'What are we accomplishing?' they asked. 'Here is this man performing many miraculous signs'" (v. 47). They cannot deny that this particular miracle is real since Lazarus had been in the grave for four days. "If we let him go on like this, everyone will believe in him" (v. 48a)—that is, they will believe in Jesus as some sort of messianic figure. That might in turn engender a political uprising against the regional superpower, the Roman Empire, and there could be only one outcome of that: "the Romans will come and take away both our place and our nation" (11:48b). The word literally rendered "place" is wonderfully ambiguous: these Jewish authorities would lose their "place" as leaders, as vassals under the superpower; i.e., they would lose their clout, authority, prestige, honor, power, and money. But in those days "our place" could refer to the temple, and hence TNIV's "the Romans will come and take away both our temple and our nation."

Caiaphas was high priest that year (v. 49). Strictly speaking, the high priest was supposed to serve for life. Annas had been appointed, but the Roman superpower kicked him out and put in his nephew or son-in-law Caiaphas (their relationship is not entirely clear). Caiaphas was high priest that fateful year, and he spoke up, "You know nothing at all!" (v. 49b). The language is derogatory: "You bunch of twits! You ignoramuses!" It is not diplomatic language at all. "You do not realize that it is better *for you* [the real locus of interest] that one man die for the people than that the whole nation perish" (v. 50). In other words, "Can't you wake up and see what is going on here? What we need is a bit of Realpolitik. What we need is a bit of crass political expediency. We've got to bump off one man, or else the whole nation is going to go, and we'll go with it. Can't you see that? What we need is a wet operation. Get this chap out of here, and we have solved the problem and saved the nation." And thus Caiaphas sacrificed judicial integrity on the altar of political expediency.

By the time John pens this account, however, both he and his readers know what happened about four decades later. The religious leaders resorted to cheap political expediency to save the nation from the ill effects they thought Jesus would bring on. The reality is that the rigged execution they helped to bring about did not save the nation, for Rome destroyed Jerusalem in A.D. 70. The authorities managed to bump off Jesus; they had him executed. And the nation died anyway. This same Jesus had cried over the city: "O Jerusalem, Jerusalem, you who kill the prophets and stone those sent to you, how often I have longed to gather your children together, as a hen gathers her chicks under her wings, and you were not willing" (Luke 13:34).

So Jesus dies—and the wretched surprise, tragic irony, is that the nation perishes anyway. Not even A.D. 70 was the end of it. Six decades later the Bar Kochba revolt brought in the Romans again (A.D. 132–135). Jerusalem was razed to the ground. It became a capital offense for any Jew to live anywhere in the environs of Jerusalem. The leaders lost their place.

But there is a second surprise, a deeper irony. Doubtless John did not see it at the time, but afterwards he saw it: Caiaphas "did not say this on his own, but as high priest that year he prophesied that Jesus would die for the Jewish nation, and not only for that nation but also for the scattered children of God, to bring them together and make them one. So from that day on they plotted to take his life" (vv. 51–53). John is not arguing that God used Caiaphas the way he used Balaam's donkey in the Old Testament (Numbers 22). God spoke to Balaam through his donkey; miraculously, the donkey spoke. But we are not to think from that narrative that the donkey was giving his considered judgment; it was a flat-out miracle. But here Caiaphas is giving his considered judgment. John is saying, "Even as Caiaphas speaks and descends to the crassness of Realpolitik, God is speaking a more profound word than Caiaphas himself could know." Caiaphas spoke of one man dying in order to save the nation, but he spoke better than he knew, for one man did die—and not only for the nation but also to gather the people of God from every tongue and tribe and people and nation into one new humanity.

Is that not what we find in the immediately preceding chapter (John 10)? Jesus calls his own sheep by name, not only out of the sheep pen of Judaism but from the other sheep pens as well: "I have other sheep that are not of this sheep pen. I must bring them also. They too will listen to my voice, and there shall be one flock and one shepherd" (v. 16). This is the case here: Jesus would die for the Jewish nation and not only for that nation but also for the scattered children of God to bring them together and make them one.

Mingled with these ironic surprises are layers of scandal. The authorities thought it scandalous that someone like Jesus should think of himself as the promised Messiah. They certainly would not have arranged to have him executed if they thought he really was the Messiah. And if they could put him down, that would prove he *could not* be the Messiah. Imagine anything as scandalous as a crucified Messiah! But the real scandal is the twisted view of political expediency they deploy to do what they think is "right." The real scandal is that by crucifying Jesus—and that for the most corrupt of motives—they serve *God's* providential purposes in slaughtering the God-man whose death accomplishes God's redemptive purposes (cf. Acts 4:27–28). As Paul would later write, "We preach Christ crucified: a stumbling block to Jews and foolishness to Gentiles, but to those whom God has called, both Jews and Greeks, Christ the power of God and the wisdom of God. For the foolishness of God is wiser than man's wisdom, and the weakness of God is stronger than man's strength" (1 Cor. 1:23–25).

Conclusion

John 11 overflows with surprises. Jesus receives a desperate plea for help and demonstrates his love—by delay (vv. 1–16). Jesus comes up against devastating loss and consoles grief—by directing attention to himself (vv. 17–27). Jesus confronts implacable death and displays his sovereignty over it—in tears and outrage (vv. 28–44). Jesus comes up against moral and spiritual death and gives life—by dying himself (vv. 45–53). And interwoven into the fabric of John's Gospel is the part this chapter plays in bringing Jesus to the cross and resurrection. Jesus heads south to Judea to raise from the dead his beloved Lazarus, and that is the trip that places him in Jerusalem during Passion Week, the week that takes him to Golgotha, the Place of the Skull. Jesus dies, and Lazarus lives—a precursor of the substitutionary death he dies for the scattered children of God. Jesus raises Lazarus from the dead, a kind of precursor to his own, more profound, resurrection—now to a newly defined resurrection existence, a new mode of life that outstrips what Lazarus has tasted.

There is a poem that summarizes so much of this, written by S. W. Gandy and often quoted:

> He death, in death, laid low;
> Made sin, he sin o'erthrew;
> Bowed to the grave, destroyed it so,
> And death, by dying, slew.

Now Thomas (called Didymus), one of the Twelve, was not with the disciples when Jesus came. So the other disciples told him, "We have seen the Lord!"

But he said to them, "Unless I see the nail marks in his hands and put my finger where the nails were, and put my hand into his side, I will not believe it."

A week later his disciples were in the house again, and Thomas was with them. Though the doors were locked, Jesus came and stood among them and said, "Peace be with you!" Then he said to Thomas, "Put your finger here; see my hands. Reach out your hand and put it into my side. Stop doubting and believe."

Thomas said to him, "My Lord and my God!"

Then Jesus told him, "Because you have seen me, you have believed; blessed are those who have not seen and yet have believed."

Jesus did many other miraculous signs in the presence of his disciples, which are not recorded in this book. But these are written that you may believe that Jesus is the Christ, the Son of God, and that by believing you may have life in his name.

—JOHN 20:24–31

5
Doubting the Resurrection of Jesus

John 20:24–31

Doubt can have so many causes.

1) For some, doubt is grounded primarily in simple ignorance. A number of years ago I served a church in Vancouver, Canada. That church had a substantial number of university students in it. One of these, a young woman with boundless energy and enthusiasm for Christ, came to me one day and said, "There's this guy at the university who has invited me out on a date to ask me some questions about Jesus. Do you think that would be okay?"

"Peggy, Peggy," I said, "be careful. Your motives may initially be excellent, but our hearts are deceitful, and pretty soon you may find yourself deeply emotionally committed to an unbeliever." She protested that there was no danger. "I don't want to compromise anything," she said. "I just want to talk to him about Jesus." We had a couple more exchanges of this sort, and then I said, slightly exasperated, "Fine! By all means go out with him. Talk to him about Jesus. And then bring him to see me."

I didn't think she'd take me literally, but that Saturday night I was in my study about 10:30 when a knock came on my door, and in bounced Peggy, with Fred behind her. "Hi," she said, "this is Fred. He wants to meet you." Well, I could see right away that that wasn't true. As far as I could tell, the only reason he wanted to see me was that I was a barrier on his way to Peggy. But we went out for a bite to eat at an all-night café. I tried to get to know him a little. He was a big man, on the football squad at the university (North American football!). He was biblically illiterate, and he was as taciturn, direct, and linear in communication as Peggy was chatty, tangential, and evocative. We were there until 1:30 AM, but I didn't think I had gotten very far.

The next Saturday night, about the same time, I heard the same knock, and in came Peggy and Fred. They had been to see a movie, and now they were seeing me. Off we went to the café. This time Fred had a list of serious questions. We started in on them. I suggested some things he should read, and we worked through some biblical passages and teachings. I returned home about 2:00 AM. The next Saturday they were back again. He had completed the readings I had assigned, and he had a new set of questions. This happened every week for about thirteen weeks. What this was doing to my Sunday morning sermons, I have no idea. But at the end of those weeks he said, "All right. I'll become a Christian."

Yes, Fred married Peggy. Today they are on the mission field. Nevertheless, I have to admit very frankly that I have seen few people become Christians in such a straightforward, linear fashion. Still, that it happens at all demonstrates that sometimes doubt and unbelief are related primarily to sheer ignorance, and the first obligation in remedying the situation is instruction.

2) Sometimes doubt is grounded in systematic moral choice. Consider the following passage from the famous writer and social cynic Aldous Huxley in his book *Ends and Means*. In this passage, Huxley unpacks themes that, historically, pushed many people to adhere to a philosophy of meaninglessness, of a valueless world:

> For myself, as, no doubt, for most of my contemporaries, the philosophy
> of meaninglessness was essentially an instrument of liberation. The lib-

eration we desired was simultaneously liberation from a certain political and economic system and liberation from a certain system of morality. We objected to the morality because it interfered with our sexual freedom; we objected to the political and economic system because it was unjust. The supporters of these systems claimed that in some way they embodied the meaning (the Christian meaning, they insisted) of the world. There was an admirably simple method of confuting these people and at the same time justifying ourselves in our political and erotic revolt: we would deny that the world had any meaning whatsoever.[1]

A little earlier in the same chapter, Huxley confesses that he himself adopted this stance for a while. He writes:

> For, like so many of my contemporaries, I took it for granted that there was no meaning [in the world]. . . . I had motives for not wanting the world to have a meaning; consequently assumed that it had none, and was able without any difficulty to find satisfying reasons for this assumption.[2]

At least this is honest, and the sentiment is not rare. For instance, I have found a similar paragraph in the writings of Michel Foucault. Here, then, is doubt sliding into systematic skepticism grounded in fundamental moral and philosophical choices.

3) Sometimes doubt is a rite of passage, a function of maturation. A child is born into and reared in a strong Christian home. Perhaps he or she attends a Christian school. Once they reach university such young people may find their ideas assaulted on so many sides that it takes a while to check the foundations. Perhaps a lecturer in sociology says, "So, Jim, you say you are a Christian. Do you come from a Christian home?"

"Yes," he replies.

---

[1]Aldous Huxley, *Ends and Means: An Enquiry into the Nature of Ideals and into the Methods Employed for Their Realization* (New York: Greenwood Press, 1937), 316.
[2]Ibid., 312.

"Do you think that a big part of why you are a Christian is because of the shaping you received in your home?"

"Of course," our Jim replies.

"Take Abdul, here. He was reared in a Muslim home. Do you think that a big part of the reason why he is a Muslim is the distinctive heritage in which he was reared?"

"Well, I suppose so."

"So if you are a Christian because of your family, and Abdul is a Muslim because of his family, who has the right to adjudicate between rival claims?"

Suddenly, on a dozen fronts, the straightforward clarity this Christian young person once enjoyed seems painfully muddied. It may take a season of doubt, wrestling, reading, talking, self-examination, even despair, before coming through to a stable stance at the other end. Granted that this is a broken world that will cough up many reasons for unbelief, surely a time of doubt can in some instances be part of a God-sanctioned process by which young Christians wrestle with how much of their belief structure is merely inherited and how much is deeply their own.

4) Sometimes doubt is generated not by a deliberate philosophical and systemic moral choice but by ten thousand atomistic choices. A man may begin his adult life with full, Christian convictions, worked out in faithful godliness, disciplined prayer and Bible reading, and thoughtful witness. Somewhere along the line, the Bible reading dries up; prayer becomes spotty; the pressures or rising obligations at work reduce church attendance to a bare minimum. A charming colleague or assistant at work seems far better able to empathize with his challenges than does his wife. Several years on, he wakes up one morning after spending the night with someone with whom he should not have been sleeping. He heads off to the washroom, looks at himself in the mirror, and mutters, "I don't believe all that religious rubbish anyway!"

But what has brought him to this point? It has not been a deeply thought-out philosophical problem, still less new scientific evidence. It has not even been a principled decision. Rather, it has been ten thousand little decisions, all of them wrong. The result is the same: this man now doubts the fundamentals of the faith.

5) Doubt may be fostered by sleep deprivation. If you keep burning the candle at both ends, sooner or later you will indulge in more and more mean cynicism—and the line between cynicism and doubt is a very thin one. Of course, different individuals require different numbers of hours of sleep; moreover, some cope with a bit of tiredness better than others. Nevertheless, if you are among those who become nasty, cynical, or even full of doubt when you are missing your sleep, you are morally obligated to try to get the sleep you need. We are whole, complicated beings: our physical existence is tied to our spiritual well-being, to our mental outlook, to our relationships with others, including our relationship with God. Sometimes the godliest thing you can do in the universe is get a good night's sleep—not pray all night, but sleep. I'm certainly not denying that there may be a place for praying all night; I'm merely insisting that in the normal course of things, spiritual discipline obligates you to get the sleep your body needs.

6) Doubt may be generated by some deep, existential crisis—the loss of a loved one, for instance, or the memory of abusive parents, or some other great suffering. Sometimes, of course, such experiences prompt the believer to put great confidence in God's providential sovereignty and goodness; at other times, believers think they are well supplied with faith until something goes wrong in their lives. Suddenly doubt leaps to life.

These six causes of doubt are not the only ones, of course; there are others. But why have I taken time to list these? The point is that just as the causes of doubt are diverse, so also are the remedies. The remedy of sleep will not help the person whose doubt is prompted by moral defection; the remedy of instruction to combat ignorance will not help the person whose doubt springs from fatigue; and so on.

So in the passage before us, we must not think that John intends to provide us with a universal answer to doubt. John here addresses the specific doubt of Thomas—so it becomes important to understand the precise nature of Thomas's doubt, or we will be expecting the passage to do something it is not designed to do. All the kinds of doubt I have listed so far surface somewhere or other in the Bible, but in this passage a particular kind of doubt is in view.

We should begin by reminding ourselves of the context in which this narrative of Thomas is set. Jesus has been crucified. Quite frankly, his own disciples had not expected this tragic turn of events. Although Jesus had spoken frequently of his impending death and subsequent resurrection, his own disciples had not understood. Perhaps they thought he was speaking in symbol-laden ways. The problem was that they had no category for a Messiah who would be crucified. Messiahs win; messiahs triumph. By the same token they had no expectation whatsoever that he would rise again from the dead. The most powerful evidence lies in the stance they adopt once Jesus is buried. They are not having a party in an upper room, quietly slapping each other on the back and exulting, "I can hardly wait until Sunday!" Rather, they find themselves in profound gloom compounded with fear that the Jewish authorities might turn on them next.

On that first resurrection Sunday the reports of the empty tomb and of the resurrection appearances began to come in. Jesus had appeared to some women. Peter and John had witnessed the empty tomb; Jesus had appeared to Peter and then to two disciples on the road to Emmaus. And then on that first Sunday evening, Jesus appeared to his apostles—but not to all twelve of them, for Judas Iscariot had committed suicide and Thomas was absent. So now we pick up the account in our text. It may be helpful to follow it in three steps.

The Cry of a Disappointed Skeptic (John 20:24–25)

The first step is the cry of a disappointed skeptic:

> Now Thomas (called Didymus), one of the Twelve, was not with the disciples when Jesus came. So the other disciples told him, "We have seen the Lord!"
>
> But he said to them, "Unless I see the nail marks in his hands and put my finger where the nails were, and put my hand into his side, I will not believe it."

So what kind of doubt is this? This is not the skepticism of the committed philosophical materialist—that is, someone who believes that all that exists is matter, energy, space, and time, and that miracles are simply impossible. Thomas, after all, was a devout first-century Jew. He believed in the God of the Bible, the God of what we call the Old Testament— and the God of the Old Testament certainly performed miracles from time to time. Nor does Thomas succumb to the doubt that springs from moral degeneration or from fatigue.

So what kind of doubt is this?

The context shows that Thomas's doubt is the skepticism of one who has gone through stupendous religious disappointment, such that he does not want to be blindsided again. Thomas had passionately believed that Jesus was the promised Messiah. Now that belief was vitiated by the barbarous crucifixion Jesus had suffered. Jesus was gone; he was dead. There was no bringing him back and no nobility in wishful thinking.

Thomas's doubt was the sort that wanted to distinguish between genuine faith and mere gullibility, the doubt that has been through profound religious disillusionment and that does not want to be snookered again.

A number of years ago there was a faith healer in California by the name of Popoff. Popoff had a habit in his ministry that soon attracted the interest of the media. Right in the middle of his meeting, he might say something like this: "The Lord is telling me, the Lord is telling me, that there is a woman in seat J42 who has severe back pain. Come forward and be healed." Sure enough, there was a woman in seat J42, and she did have back pain. Some media people interviewed these folk, but they could not find a single one who would admit to collusion.

Eventually an ABC television crew went into one of these meetings not only with a tiny video camera but with a radio scanner. They had noticed that Popoff had a hearing aid, and they had their suspicions. (What a faith healer is doing with a hearing aid is a separate question I will not attempt to explore.) It turned out that when people poured into the great hall, attendants encouraged them to fill out cards detailing their prayer requests. Among these attendants was Mrs. Popoff. When someone wrote on one of these cards that he or she was suffering from, say, a vicious melanoma and had only months to live, the card was jettisoned. By contrast, if someone wrote that he or she was suffering from something that had at least a good chance of being at least partly psychosomatic, like back pain, Mrs. Popoff noted where the person sat and wrote, for example, "Woman. J42. Severe back pain." Then, in the midst of the service, she would radio down to her husband. Popoff would pick up her signal by the device in his ear, which was not really a hearing aid but a radio receiver. He might hear his wife say, in effect, "Dear, we've got one. There's a woman in seat J42 with severe back pain." The audience would hear only the words of Popoff himself: "The Lord is telling me, the Lord is telling me, that there is a woman in seat J42 who has severe back pain. Come forward and be healed." On national television, the ABC television crew played what the scene looked like from the perspective of the audience filling the hall, and then played it again dubbing in the signal from Mrs. Popoff. I cannot resist saying that, at least for a while, Popoff's ministry popped off.

Now why do I tell you this story? I am certainly not saying that God cannot perform a miracle of healing if he chooses to do so. Nor is this to assert that all faith healers are charlatans and tricksters. The reason I tell you this story is to point out that doubtless many of the thousands of people who were swept up in Popoff's ministry were Christians—but Christians who were frankly naive. They were snookered by Popoff's scheme; they were unable to distinguish between genuine faith and sheer gullibility. So eager were they to believe in the miraculous that, quite frankly, they were foolish and gullible.

Thomas did not want to belong to the number of the gullible. So what he asks for in this passage is the most personal and concrete demonstration he can think of, something that would prove that this ostensible resurrected apparition has genuine, physical continuity with the Jesus who was put into the tomb. There needs to be convincing evidence that the Jesus who died was in genuine continuity with the ostensible resurrected Jesus. Thomas does not want to be deceived by, say, an identical twin who conveniently pops up. So he says, "Unless I see the nail marks in his hands and put my finger where the nails were, and put my hand into his side, I will not believe it" (v. 25).

The Romans deployed three methods of execution; crucifixion was by far the cruelest. It was reserved for slaves, scumbags, traitors. No Roman citizen could be executed by crucifixion except by the explicit sanction of the emperor himself. The victim was tied or nailed to a cross.

There he pulled with his arms and pushed with his legs so as to keep his chest cavity open in order to breathe. Pretty soon he was wracked with muscle spasms, and collapsed in agony. But then he needed to breathe, so he pulled with his arms and pushed with his legs, and the cycle started again. This could go on for days, until eventually the victim died of suffocation. If for some reason the soldiers wanted to finish off their victims more quickly—for instance, if there was a holy day coming, and the bodies had to be taken down from the cross and buried, as in this case—they would simply smash the shin bones of the victim. The victim could no longer push with his legs, and he would suffocate quickly.

But when they came to Jesus, they found him already dead. Instead of breaking his legs, one of the soldiers shoved his short spear up under Jesus' rib cage, piercing the pericardium, causing blood and water to flow out of his side. That meant that Jesus' body, carefully laid in the tomb of Joseph of Arimathea, had unique wounds. Thomas knew it. That is why he demanded to see and touch not only the wounds in Jesus' hands and feet, but the wound in his side. He wanted to be sure, beyond all possibility of ambiguity, hallucination, or trickery, that this ostensible resurrected Jesus had genuine continuity with the dead Jesus who was taken down from the tomb. Only that would overcome his doubt, he insists, for he does not want to succumb to mere gullibility.

Perhaps, too, Thomas demanded so much because he found it difficult to imagine how the genuine Messiah could have been made to suffer such shame. Crucifixion was not only physically agonizing, but it was associated in the ancient world with the most horrific degradation and shame. It was going to take pretty remarkable evidence to convince Thomas that Jesus was truly the Messiah he had hoped for all along—and now risen again, alive, triumphant.

Here, then, is the cry of a disappointed skeptic.

The Adoration of an Astonished Skeptic
(John 20:26–28)

The second step is the adoration of an astonished skeptic:

> A week later his disciples were in the house again, and Thomas was with them. Though the doors were locked, Jesus came and stood among them and said, "Peace be with you!" Then he said to Thomas, "Put your finger here; see my hands. Reach out your hand and put it into my side. Stop doubting and believe."
>
> Thomas said to him, "My Lord and my God!"

The text tells us that this scene takes place the next week, that is, the second Sunday after the resurrection. The circumstances are similar: the apostles are in a house, meeting in a room with locked doors. As he had the first Sunday, Jesus suddenly appeared among them. This was not something he ever did, so far as the records go, before his resurrection. Again, as he did the first Sunday, Jesus greets them with the same greeting: "Peace be with you!" At a superficial level, this is probably simply "Shalom!"—the Hebrew equivalent of modern Arabic's "Salaam!" Yet the word *shalom* often connotes total well-being before God. The word in this context may be pregnant with eschatological expectation: this side of Jesus' cross and resurrection, men and women may truly enjoy the ultimate reconciliation, peace with God himself, in anticipation of perfect peace with God on the last day.

But Jesus' next words are what grab our attention. He turns to Thomas, and, even though he had not been physically present to hear Thomas's robust challenge, Jesus knows what evidence Thomas demands, and so he says to him, "Put your finger here; see my hands. Reach out your hand and put it into my side. Stop doubting and believe" (v. 27).

And Thomas says to him, "My Lord and my God!" (v. 28).

This is a stunning confession. In some ways it brings out, toward the end of the book, what John the Evangelist has already asserted in the very first verse of his Gospel: "In the beginning was the Word, and the Word was with God, *and the Word was God*" (1:1). We must not skip over the confession too quickly. There are depths to be plumbed here, depths that are interpretative, historical, and theological, before we press on to the closing verses of the chapter. I would like to mention four.

1) Most of us, I suspect, are aware that friendly neighborhood Jehovah's Witnesses find it difficult to accept this verse at face value. They do not believe that Jesus is truly God; he is, at best, a junior god. They therefore offer two quite different interpretations of verse 28 in order to domesticate it and make it come out with a meaning congruent with their understanding of Christ. I shall mention only one of these two interpretations. They suggest that what Thomas said, in an ejaculation of sheer surprise, was, in effect, "My Lord! My God!"

It is difficult to take this interpretation seriously. It would mean that Thomas's first response to seeing and being invited to touch the resurrected Jesus was blasphemy. Every culture, of course, develops its own forms of vulgarity, profanity, and blasphemy. But it is just about unthinkable to imagine that a devout Jew like Thomas would take on his lips the word "God" as a profane exclamation. But worse, even if we could somehow imagine that Thomas would blaspheme in this way, it would then seem that Jesus approves the blasphemy, since he approves Thomas's words in the next verse. Above all, the little word "and" stands against this interpretation. Even if we could somehow imagine that Thomas could blaspheme by saying "My Lord! My God!" it is simply ridiculous to suppose that the blasphemy uttered was "My Lord *and* my God!"

No, the text must be taken at face value. Thomas, a first-century monotheistic Jew, addresses Jesus, the resurrected Jesus, with the stunning confession, "My Lord and my God." That brings us to the second matter to consider.

2) If Thomas's confession is read in context, it is, quite frankly, initially astonishing. Why does he confess so much? Unlike his earlier skepticism, he now knows that Jesus has returned from the dead. He sees the wounds and is assured that the Jesus before him has continuity with the Jesus who was taken down from the cross and laid in the tomb. So why does he not simply exclaim, "Jesus, you *are* alive!" Or even, "Oops!" On first reading, we cannot help but wonder what drove Thomas to this sweeping conclusion, which seems more than the immediate context warrants.

We must place Thomas within the framework of the larger narrative of John's Gospel. An entire week passes between verse 25 and verse 26. Verse 26 carefully notes that Jesus appeared to Thomas a week after Thomas had expressed his doubt. One can easily imagine the nature of the probing reflections that occupied his mind and imagination throughout that week: "Jesus alive? It can't be! But the other ten are so very sure. They simply have to be mistaken. But suppose they're not? Is it possible that Jesus really is alive? What would that mean? No, it can't be. I need some evidence. He can't possibly be alive. But suppose that he is?"

In the matrix of such mental wrestling, he could not help but remember the strange words that Jesus had said just a few days earlier, the night that he was betrayed, condemned, and crucified. Jesus had said to one of them in the hearing of all, "Don't you know me, Philip, even after I have been among you such a long time? Anyone who has seen me has seen the Father" (John 14:9). Doubtless, at the time, Thomas and the others heard this as just one more enigmatic utterance of Jesus that still did not make too much sense. But if Jesus really *had* arisen from the dead, would not such utterances provoke renewed reflection about what Jesus was claiming? "Anyone who has seen me has seen the Father"—what a massive claim. Indeed, John's Gospel preserves an array of other equally startling claims found on the lips of Jesus. For instance, Jesus insists that God has entrusted all judgment into Jesus' hands, in order that "all may honor the Son just as they honor the Father" (John 5:23). Elsewhere, Jesus declares, "Before Abraham was born, I am" (John 8:58); again, "Whatever the Father does the Son also does" (John 5:19). On the face of it, the claims were stupendous. This side of the resurrection, Thomas is doubtless forced to think about them more deeply than he has to this point.

All of this falls right out of the narrative text of the fourth Gospel. John's Gospel provides the narrative matrix in which Thomas's mental wrestlings take place during that week, bounded at one end by his articulation of doubt in Jesus' resurrection and at the other end by his confession, "My Lord and my God!" But there are two larger contexts we must not ignore. The *first* of these is the other canonical Gospels. Thomas was present not only for the incidents already referred to in the Gospel of John but also for other incidents recorded only in the Synoptic Gospels. Let me mention only one of them. You will recall what takes place in Mark 2 when Jesus was preaching in a house packed full of eager hearers. A paralyzed man was carried to the house on some kind of litter, some kind of bed or mattress, by four of his friends who hoped that Jesus would heal their friend. Those listening to Jesus tried to shoo them away: "Shhh! Jesus is speaking! Be quiet! Wait your turn!" Desperate to find help for their paralyzed friend, the four carry him up onto the flat roof (a very common construction at the time), carefully listen for Jesus' voice, and remove the tiles over the place where Jesus was speaking. They then lower their paralyzed friend down in front of Jesus. As for the crowd, if it will not make way, out of courtesy and compassion, for the paralytic when he is at the door and his friends are trying to get him in to see Jesus, they now make way for him, to avoid the bed coming down on their heads.

Jesus looks at the paralyzed man and tells him, "Your sins are forgiven" (Mark 2:5). Immediately some of the Jewish theologians in attendance are quietly outraged, muttering to one another, "Who can forgive
sins but God alone?" Their rhetorical question is hugely important and
deserves further reflection.

Toward the end of World War II, Simon Wiesenthal was in a work
gang in the horrific concentration camp at Auschwitz. All his relatives
had been killed. Wiesenthal did not then know that he was only weeks
from being rescued by the Russians who would shortly reach the camp
and free it. On this particular day, Wiesenthal was pulled out of the
work gang and shoved into a room where he found a young German
soldier, perhaps nineteen years old, severely wounded and clearly dying.
The young German had asked to talk with a Jew before he died—and
in the peculiar providence of God, Wiesenthal was the one who was
shoved into the room with him. The dying German soldier was frankly
terrified in the face of his impending death. He knew he would shortly
face God. He knew something of what Nazis had done to Jews; he knew
some things that he himself had done to Jews. Staring eternity in the face,
the young German soldier asked Wiesenthal for forgiveness, treating
Wiesenthal, in effect, as a representative Jew.

Wiesenthal agonized over the desperate request. His reasoning, in
brief, was this: surely only the offended party has a right to forgive. How
can those who have not suffered extend forgiveness on behalf of those
who have? Since most of the victims of the Nazis were killed, Wiesenthal
argued to himself, how can those still living extend forgiveness on behalf
of the slain? *So there is no forgiveness for the Nazis!* In that little room
with the dying Nazi soldier, Wiesenthal worked this all out in his mind,
and then, without saying a word, he simply turned and left the room.
After the war was over, Wiesenthal wrote up his experience in a memo-

rable little book titled *The Sunflower: On the Possibilities and Limits of Forgiveness*.[3] Many of its pages are given over to Wiesenthal's internal agonizing as he weighed the request of this young Nazi soldier. He sent his work to many of the world's leading ethicists and asked them the question, "Was I right? Was I right to behave as I did?"

Well, was he? Surely we cannot take issue with his insight that only the offended party has the right to forgive. Do you recall the illustration I used in chapter 2, in connection with Romans 3:21–26? The same illustration speaks powerfully to *this* situation as well, so let me remind you of the crucial point. Suppose on your way home from a meeting you are attacked, brutalized, perhaps gang-raped, and left for dead. Suppose, further, that tomorrow I go and visit you in the hospital. Suppose, too, that by some amazing fluke I've found your attackers, so when I see you in the hospital, I say to you, "Take courage! You will be greatly relieved to learn that I have found your attackers, *and I have forgiven them!*" What will you say to me? I suspect you will sputter in fury and outrage, "Who do you think you are? *You're* not the one lying here in a body cast! *You* weren't gang-raped! *You* haven't had half the bones in your body broken! What on earth gives *you* the right to think *you* can forgive *anybody* for what was done *to me?*"

And, of course, you'd be right, just as Wiesenthal was right; only the offended party can forgive the offense. Yet there was one additional detail that Wiesenthal left out of his calculations, a detail that the Bible makes very clear. Do you recall the rather grim account of how King David seduced a young wife next door, while her husband was away at the front, fighting David's wars? I referred to it in the second chapter of this book; I want now to return to it one last time. The woman, Bathsheba, soon discovered she was pregnant and let David know. As commander-in-chief, David arranged for the young husband to come

---

[3]New York: Schocken, 1997.

home, ostensibly bearing a communication from the commanders at the front for David. David assumed the man, whose name was Uriah, would go home and sleep with his wife before returning to the battle lines, but this remarkable young man so empathized with his mates who were still on the front line that he did not even check in at home. Why should he enjoy the pleasures of home when his mates couldn't? So King David knew that he was snookered. He sent Uriah back to the front, carrying a secret message to the unit commander. The commander was to arrange a skirmish in which everyone in the unit would know about a secret signal to fall back at a set time—everyone, that is, except this young husband, Uriah the Hittite. The inevitable happened: the skirmish grew warm, the signal was given, and everyone fell back except Uriah, who was left at the sharp end. He was killed. After a barely decent interval, David married Bathsheba and thought he had gotten away with it.

Eventually, however, he is confronted by Nathan the prophet. You might fool a lot of people when you sin, but you never fool God. As Hebrews 4:13 puts it, "Everything is uncovered and laid bare before the eyes of him to whom we must give account." God knows what David has done, he lets his prophet Nathan know, and Nathan confronts David. I do not have time to remind you of everything that happened in the wake of that confrontation. But one of the most remarkable psalms ever written was penned by David after he had repented in desperate tears for all the sin he had committed. In that psalm, Psalm 51, David addresses God, and he says, "Against you, you only, have I sinned and done what is evil in your sight" (Ps. 51:4).

A superficial reading of these words might prompt us to think that David is utterly mistaken: he seems to have sinned against just about everyone. Yet at a deep level, what David writes is exactly true. What makes sin *sin*, what makes it so profoundly heinous, what makes it so deeply repugnant and culpable, is that it is offense against God. We dare not forget that the first commandment, according to Jesus, is the commandment to love God with heart and soul and mind and strength. Thus the first sin—first sequentially, first in fundamental importance—is *not* to love God with heart and soul and mind and strength. It is the sin we always commit when we commit any other sin. At the most profound level, whenever we sin, God is the most offended party. If, like David, we commit adultery, God is the most offended party. If we cheat on our income taxes, God is the most offended party. If we puff ourselves up in pride, indulge in slander, demean a colleague, or nurture bitterness, God is the most offended party. If we watch porn on the internet, God is the most offended party. David understands this: "Against you, you only, have I sinned and done what is evil in your sight." *And that is why, whatever other forgiveness we try to secure, we must have God's forgiveness, or we have nothing.* Yes, you and I need to forgive one another. Yet in the most profound analysis of what sin is, only God can forgive sin.

And here is Jesus forgiving this paralyzed man his sin. "Who can forgive sins but God alone?" some in the crowd asked.

Who, indeed? Jesus' words are surely the raving remarks of a megalomaniac who thinks of himself as God. Or—is it possible?—Jesus really is God.

And Thomas was there.

Or perhaps during the week between the Sunday when Thomas expressed his doubt and the Sunday when Jesus appeared once again inside a locked room, Thomas recalled a still larger context. Perhaps he let his mind roam over some Old Testament Scriptures that began to blossom with new meaning. Doubtless Thomas knew words that we Christians today recite every Christmas: "For to us a child is born, to us a son is given, and the government will be on his shoulders" (Isa. 9:6). On the one hand the prophet Isaiah writes, more than seven hundred years before Christ, "Of the increase of his government and peace there will be no end. He will reign on David's throne and over his kingdom" (v. 7); but Isaiah also says, in the same context, "And he will be called Wonderful Counselor, Mighty God, Everlasting Father, Prince of Peace" (v. 6).

How does one put all such pieces together? Thomas had an entire week to mull the matter over. Doubtless he still could not put together what would later be called the doctrine of the Trinity. But he had progressed far enough in his understanding to grasp that if Jesus was truly alive, this was more, even, than a spectacular resurrection: it was the visitation of God Almighty.

3) Perhaps that is as much as we can say about Thomas's beliefs. There is not enough evidence to warrant assertions that at this early date he also thought through the implications of asserting that the one whom he confessed as "Lord" and "God" had actually died. And what a death: by crucifixion, condemned by the Roman government, hanging from a tree under God's curse, and yet transparently vindicated by being raised from the dead. But even if we cannot be quite certain how much Thomas himself understood at this turning point in his life, we are on much more solid ground when we reflect on what the evangelist John understood when, some decades later, he reported these events by writing this book. For John has already announced that Jesus is the Lamb of God who takes away the sin of the world (1:29). He has likened Jesus to the serpent hanging on a pole for the saving of the people of God after their horrific rebellion and the onset of the curse that fell on them (3:14, referring to Numbers 21). He likens Jesus to bread: either the grain dies so that people may live, or, if nothing dies to provide human beings with life, the

people themselves must die. John reports that under God's providential hand, even the high priest Caiaphas speaks prophetically, in words more pregnant with meaning than Caiaphas himself can understand, when he asserts that Jesus must die so that the people of God will not perish; what Caiaphas wants is a substitute death, and he gets more than he expected (11:49–51). Jesus is like a kernel of wheat (12:23–24) which, if it dies, is multiplied in the new life that springs forth.

So when John reports these words of Thomas's, "My Lord and my God!" he cannot help but see that there is a marvel on top of a marvel. Two thousand years later, we who read John's words observe not only the mind-bending notion of the incarnation, God becoming a human being, but the utterly shattering fact that this God-man died a substitutionary death, the death of a redeeming lamb. It is staggering to contemplate the God of the Bible becoming a man; it is even more staggering to contemplate him as he dies our death—and is then vindicated in resurrection. Yes, yes, no lesser words of acclamation will do: "My Lord and my God!" The confession is scandalous; the confession is glorious.

The closing months of World War I, that bloodiest and most stupid of wars, witnessed the rise of a number of important poets whose work reflected on the war. One of the minor poets of this group was Edward Shillito. Although the body of his work is not particularly distinguished, his poem "Jesus of the Scars" is immortal. In two of the verses of that poem he uses language that recalls this occasion in John 20 when Jesus appears in a room with locked doors. Shillito writes:

If when the doors are shut, thou drawest near,
Only reveal thy hands, that side of thine.
We know today what wounds are, never fear:
Show us thy wounds: we know the countersign.

The other gods were strong, but thou wast weak.
They rode, but thou didst stumble to thy throne.
And to our wounds, only God's wounds can speak—
And not a god has wounds, but thou alone.

All this, transparently, the evangelist John understood.

4) We must also reflect on the repeated little word "my." Thomas does not say, "Our Lord and our God," as if he were reciting some sort of liturgical slogan. His confession is intensely personal: "*My* Lord and *my* God!" It is never enough merely to confess the truth of something that is out there in the public arena. Even the Devil himself could affirm, however begrudgingly, that Jesus is both Lord and God. But a true child of God is making more than a public statement about a public truth. The Christian is not simply affirming that Jesus Christ is the Lord and God of the universe but that in the most intimate sense he is the Christian's Lord and God. The confession is intensely personal. If you cannot utter the words of this confession with similar deeply personal commitment, you have no part of Jesus and the salvation that flows from his death and resurrection. Your heart and mind must confess with wonder, "My Lord and my God!"

These, then, are four reflections that flow from the adoration of this astonished skeptic.

The Function of a Converted Skeptic (John 20:29–31)

The third step is the function of a converted skeptic:

> Then Jesus told him, "Because you have seen me, you have believed; blessed are those who have not seen and yet have believed."
>
> Jesus did many other miraculous signs in the presence of his disciples, which are not recorded in this book. But these are written that you may believe that Jesus is the Christ, the Son of God, and that by believing you may have life in his name.

I suspect that verse 29 is frequently misunderstood. Quite mistakenly, some think that Jesus is saying that faith not based in signs, and perhaps not based in truth, is superior faith. It is as if Jesus were saying, "Well, all right, Thomas, now that you've seen me, you have believed. Fair enough. So now you have faith. But you must understand that those who believe in me even though they never have enjoyed the signs given to you have a superior faith; they are truly blessed. You missed out on that, Thomas, because you insisted on seeing before believing. Your faith is at best second-class faith."

I must say, as strongly as I can, that verse 29 cannot legitimately be interpreted that way. The reason we are tempted to misinterpret verse 29 in that way is that in much of contemporary Western culture the word *faith* has come to have meanings it never has in the Bible. In our world, the word *faith* tends to mean one of two things. First, it may function as a synonym for *religion*; that is, there are many "faiths," there are many "religions." Second, more commonly it means something like "a personal, subjective, private, religious choice or commitment." In other words, it has nothing to do with facts or historical realities; it is a personal, subjective, private, religious choice. You have your faith, and I have mine, and it is impossible to adjudicate the disparities between your faith and mine because there are no hard data to enable us to draw intelligent comparisons.

Indeed, it is not uncommon for people to feel superior because they *believe* something; they have *faith* in something, for which there is *no* justifiable support. This understanding of faith is well exemplified in the book by Dan Brown, *The Da Vinci Code*. In that book, Sophie exclaims to the hero, Langdon, "But you told me the New Testament is based on fabrication." Langdon replies, "Sophie, *every* faith in the world is based on fabrication. That is the definition of *faith*—acceptance of that which we imagine to be true, that which we cannot prove." Certainly *some* objects of faith in the Bible, matters disclosed by revelation, cannot in any sense be "proved," but other objects of faith in the Bible are disclosed in the matrix *of history*. In such cases we have access to these historical claims by the same means by which we have access to *any* history, namely, witness.

But if "faith" *means* that there is no access to verifying *any* of faith's objects, if faith *means* that fabrication of faith's objects is part of the game, then verse 29 is readily misinterpreted: that faith is superior that has nothing to support it! That faith is superior that desires no evidence! That faith is superior that doesn't care about whether Jesus *actually* rose from the dead. If you *believe* he rose from the dead, that is enough; that is what makes it genuine faith, God-blessed faith. Indeed, I have heard distinguished clerics say that if Jesus' tomb were found, with the body still in it, and virtually no doubt that the body truly is that of Jesus, their Christian faith would not be at all troubled. After all, they say, Jesus has risen in their hearts.

The apostle Paul certainly did not see things that way. Writing to the Corinthians, he argues that if Jesus has *not* risen from the dead, while you believe that he *has* risen from the dead, then your faith in Jesus' resurrection is futile; it is worthless. In other words, one of the things that validates faith is the truthfulness of faith's object. Faith is *more* than believing the truth, of course; after all, the demons themselves believe that Jesus rose from the dead, but that doesn't do them any good. But although saving faith is *more* than believing the truth, it is never less. That is why the Bible never urges us to believe something that is not true, or something that may not be true. It is also why, in the Bible, one of the crucial ways by which we strengthen faith is by articulating and defending the truth.

But once we have successfully eliminated a false interpretation of John 20:29, what this verse means becomes readily transparent. John closely links verse 29 with verses 30 and 31. The flow of thought then runs like this: John reports that Jesus says to Thomas, in effect, "Thomas, you have seen, and you have believed." All along, of course, John's Gospel has taught that believing in Jesus is necessary if a person is to have eternal life. Many chapters earlier we read the words, "For God so loved the world that he gave his one and only Son, that whoever *believes* in him . . . [may] have *eternal life*" (3:16)—so of course it is wonderful to see that Thomas truly believes. But Jesus knows, as John knows, that many people will come to put their faith in Jesus who have never seen the resurrected Jesus as Thomas did. Jesus will ascend and not be physically available until his return. Yet countless millions will come to believe that he rose from the dead. They were never invited to touch the wounds as Thomas was; they never saw the resurrected Jesus eat fish on the shores of Galilee as did the seven disciples described in John 21. On what basis, then, will they believe? Jesus says that those who have not seen and yet have believed are blessed. Why? Because they have believed without any evidence at all? No, of course not.

John immediately goes on to say that Jesus did many miraculous signs, and of course they could not all be written down for us. But these are written, the ones in John's Gospel, *including the appearance to Thomas*, in order that later generations who will never *see* the signs, who will not in this life *see* the resurrected body of Jesus, might believe that Jesus is the Messiah, the Son of God, and that by believing they might have life through his name. The means by which we believers of later generations have access to the historical witnesses of the resurrected Jesus is through the written records the first generation left behind. Thus Thomas becomes part of this chain of evidence, this chain of attestation. He saw and believed, and by his witness, by his confession, recorded in this book, he still speaks and, by God's grace, generates faith in countless later generations who come to share his faith because of his witness to the truth. Like Thomas, because of Thomas, they believe, they have eternal life, and they are blessed.

Thomas begins as a skeptic; he continues in personal adoration when his doubts are overcome by the appearance of the Lord Jesus; and now he functions as part of the chain of witnesses who call forth faith in the Lord Jesus, among generations yet unborn. Just as Peter, in John 21, is restored to the Savior and to useful, lifelong service after his terrible betrayal of Jesus, so Thomas, here in John 20, is restored not only to faith but to useful, ages-long witness to the truth, to the One who is the truth, after his painful doubt. His confession and witness come down to us in the words of Holy Scripture, and by God's mercy, countless millions who have never seen the resurrected Jesus as Thomas saw him, believe and are blessed. Here is the function of a converted skeptic.

Conclusion

In the most profound sense, of course, it would be wrong to end this chapter by talking about Thomas. For although these verses, at one level, can truly be said to be about Thomas, they are, of course, more deeply about the resurrected Jesus. Indeed, this narrative is embedded in a book we call "a gospel." More accurately, it is the Gospel of Jesus Christ according to John. This gospel, this good news of Jesus Christ according to Matthew, Mark, Luke, and John, is irreducibly bound up with Jesus' person and work, with his reign and his cross, with his death and his resurrection. And where men and women across the ages, whether in Bible times or in our times, come to believe, truly believe, that Jesus rose from the dead to be Lord and Savior, utterly vindicated by his heavenly Father, they find it changes everything. That is one of the great lessons of all the resurrection accounts:

> They came alone: some women who remembered him,
> Bowed down with spices to anoint his corpse.
> Through darkened streets, they wept their way to honor him—
> The one whose death had shattered all their hopes.

Why do you look for life among these tombs of stone?
He is not here. He's risen, as he said.
Remember how he spoke to you in Galilee:
"The Son of Man must die—and must rise up from the dead."

The two walked home, a portrait of defeat and loss,
Explaining to a stranger why the gloom—
How Jesus seemed to be the King before his cross;
Now all their hopes lay buried in his tomb.
"How slow you are to see. Didn't this have to be?
Don't you believe the words the prophets said?
Christ had to suffer first, then enter glory."
Then he unveiled their eyes in the breaking of the bread.

He heard their words, but not for him that easy faith
That trades the truth for sentimental sigh.
Unless he saw the nail marks in his hands himself,
And touched his side, he'd not believe the lie.
Then Jesus came to them, although the doors were locked:
"Cast away doubt and reach into my side.
Trace out the wounds the nails left in my broken hands,
And understand I am the resurrection and the life."

Long years have passed, and still we fear the face of death;
It steals our loved ones, leaving us undone.
It mocks our dreams and calls to us with icy breath,
The final terror when life's course is run.
But this I know: my Lord traveled this way before,
His body clothed in immortality.
The sepulcher's sting is drawn, the power of sin destroyed.
Death has been swallowed up in his mighty victory.[4]

---

[4]D. A. Carson, "They Came Alone," track 5, in *For the Love of God*, vol. 2 of New Songs for the People of God (2005).

General Index

Scripture Index

 RE:LIT

Resurgence Literature (Re:Lit) is a ministry of the Resurgence. At www.theResurgence.com you will find free theological resources in blog, audio, video, and print forms, along with information on forthcoming conferences, to help Christians contend for and contextualize Jesus' gospel. At www.ReLit.org you will also find the full lineup of Resurgence books for sale. The elders of Mars Hill Church have generously agreed to support Resurgence and the Acts 29 Church Planting Network in an effort to serve the entire church.

FOR MORE RESOURCES

Re:Lit – www.relit.org
Resurgence – www.theResurgence.com
Re:Sound – www.resound.org
Mars Hill Church – www.marshillchurch.org
Acts 29 – www.acts29network.org